THE NIQAB IN FRANCE

The Niqab in France

BETWEEN PIETY AND SUBVERSION

Agnès De Féo

TRANSLATED BY LINDSAY TURNER

FORDHAM UNIVERSITY PRESS   NEW YORK   2024

This work received support for excellence in publication and translation from Albertine Translation, a program created by Villa Albertine and funded by FACE Foundation.

This book was first published in French as *Derrière le niqab: 10 ans d'enquête sur les femmes qui ont porté et enlevé le voile intégral*, by Agnès De Féo © Armand Colin 2020, Malakoff. ARMAND COLIN is a trademark of DUNOD Editeur - 11, rue Paul Bert - 92240 MALAKOFF.

This work, published as part of a program of aid for publication, received support from the Institut Français.

Copyright © 2024 Fordham University Press

All rights reserved. No part of this publication may be reproduced, stored in a retrieval system, or transmitted in any form or by any means—electronic, mechanical, photocopy, recording, or any other—except for brief quotations in printed reviews, without the prior permission of the publisher.

Fordham University Press has no responsibility for the persistence or accuracy of URLs for external or third-party Internet websites referred to in this publication and does not guarantee that any content on such websites is, or will remain, accurate or appropriate.

Fordham University Press also publishes its books in a variety of electronic formats. Some content that appears in print may not be available in electronic books.

Visit us online at www.fordhampress.com.

Library of Congress Cataloging-in-Publication Data available online at https://catalog.loc.gov.

Printed in the United States of America

26 25 24   5 4 3 2 1

First edition

Contents

PREFACE TO THE ENGLISH-LANGUAGE EDITION   vii

A NOTE ON TERMINOLOGY   xi

PART I

Introduction   3

The Sociology of Niqab Wearers   17

The Niqab and the Other   35

A Reaction to the Ban   49

Conclusion   65

PART II

16 Portraits of Women Wearing the Niqab   71

Earlier Wearers (Before 2009),   71

Neo-Niqab Wearers (After 2009),   101

The Niqab: Refuting Common Ideas   155

ACKNOWLEDGMENTS   163

NOTES   165

SELECTED BIBLIOGRAPHY AND FILMOGRAPHY   171

Preface to the English-Language Edition
By Agnès De Féo

Thanks to Lindsay Turner's translation of my book, English-speaking readers will get a new look at a phenomenon that is, to say the least, controversial. This book is about women who wore the niqab (full-face veil) during the decade following the passage of the 2010 law banning the garment in public spaces in France. My research has shown me that this law did not have the desired effect. Far from eliminating the niqab's presence in public spaces (which was already rare), the law has actually increased it. For some women, the ban has made the niqab attractive as a form of subversion, worn for self-assertion and in opposition to or protest against society; for some, it has become a form of resistance against the sexualization, objectification, and commodification of the female body. Because wearing the niqab goes against most conventions of female attractiveness, it might even be seen to represent the refusal of feminine beauty norms as dictated by the fashion industry. This is all the more unexpected when we consider the general profile of my interviewees, many of whom previously held jobs in the beauty industry. Abused, disillusioned, bruised, these women reappropriate a radical symbol in order to fight against a society perceived as sexist.

My objective in this book is to present a nuanced and complex picture of the niqab in France today by entering into the subjectivities of the women who wear it. When I began my study in France in 2008, I faced opposition in the French academic world. Some of my fellow researchers questioned my research results, which seemed counterintuitive, accusing me of lacking objectivity. At the time, a woman wearing the niqab voluntarily was unimaginable for a large segment of the French population, including researchers.

In France, the Muslim veil is omnipresent in the news, in various contexts: in schools, worn by students or their mothers, at work, at the beach, at the swimming pool. It is a subject regularly brought to public attention by opinion makers, the media, and politicians seeking to gain support by raising the specter of the Islamization of society. Minor controversies quickly escalate into national causes. The French pillar of secularism is often weaponized against what remains the expression of religious freedom, guaranteed by the constitution.

The general public, which most often has no interaction at all with veiled women, tends to project onto them fantasies that are based not on reality but on myths inherited from orientalism and colonialism. Women wearing the niqab are accused of perpetuating patriarchal customs that position them as inferior to men. In this view, they are subjugated to Muslim men and need, even against their will, to be freed. But the problem goes deeper: the niqab (and the veil in general) is perceived as a danger to social cohesion. Women who wear it are accused of undermining "living together," an expression frequently invoked by the opponents of the niqab and supporters of the ban, and of inciting "separatism." In the social imaginary, they are the embodiment of the "Islamization" of French society, a threat inherent in the concept of the "great replacement" that is promoted by extreme right-wing groups, as well as by some on the left. The conflation of the veil and radical Islamism is taken as a given.

My extensive research over the past fifteen years has led me to perceive new and surprising sides of the niqab. Through empirical work, based on participant observation, I have maintained trusting relationships with women wearing the niqab in order to access their intimate spheres and understand their motivations. By becoming a part of their lives, I have been able to collect testimonies, confessions, and revelations.

It is worth emphasizing that in France, the niqab is an individual phenomenon; it is not linked to any tradition or to family pressure. Niqab wearers do not belong to traditional re-Islamization movements, such as Tablighi or the Muslim Brotherhood. They are most often unaware of the ideological struggles of political Islam, but instead refer to Salafi ideology as a source of personal development. They wear religious attire as a personal choice. Often, they are girls and young women dissatisfied with the construction of the female body in the modern world.

In France, women wearing the niqab are far removed from the traditional Muslim model centered on family, children, and the seclusion of women in the home. Far from being invisible, they want to be seen. They publicly claim their particularism in a form of exhibitionism that paradoxically claims to be modesty. Some Salafi Muslim women have reinvested Western feminist discourse with new meaning in order to make their voices heard in the battle for public opinion that surrounded the vote banning the garment in 2010. These young women, covering their faces, might be considered the unlikely heirs of

Western feminists, claiming control over their bodies, against a masculine order. They are quick to claim the feminist slogan: "My body belongs to me." They share some of the same characteristics: matrimonial independence, freedom to change partners, etc. Frequently dissatisfied, they initiate romantic breakups often. Women who wear the niqab manage to handle two, apparently contradictory, ideologies: rigorous Islam and feminism. In so doing, they offer a chance to look at both again.

Another fact that undermines received ideas: the majority of niqab wearers are converts to Islam, most often from the middle class, in search of a subversive identity, both conforming to a Muslim ideal and undertaking an anti-social move against their parents. Contrary to those women who wear the hijab and who tend to seek integration into the workforce, women who wear the niqab want to distinguish themselves and demonstrate their determination. They have attempted to turn the niqab into a counterculture, even to the point of complete isolation from society. But since the publication of this book, in France at the end of 2020, the niqab has become less and less common, due in part to images of female jihadists captured in Syria, including Émilie König, whose profile is given in Part Two of this book. Images of women wearing the niqab in prison camps have tarnished, or at least complicated, the image of the rebel.

For ten years, the idea that a face-to-face encounter is necessary for communication with others (to cite the philosopher Emmanuel Levinas) has been repeated like a mantra against the niqab. Yet this argument quickly broke down when the mask became mandatory during the COVID-19 pandemic. Alleged communication problems were glossed over. The mask became a matter of course for protection. But the niqab has never been seen as protection, an argument that some women, in fact, invoke when they say that they "feel better and protected" wearing it. Instead of liberating women, the law has bruised them, caused them unnecessary suffering, and put them in danger: they were targeted by racist threats and violence, as well as police controls that were often traumatic in the presence of their children. And ironically, history has proven them right. Exactly ten years after the vote of the ban in France, during the height of the COVID-19 pandemic, covering one's face became compulsory, while both the traditional French greeting of a kiss on the cheek, and the greeting of a handshake, were forbidden (the refusal to shake hands with the opposite sex is part of the grievances against Muslims accused of lacking "savoir vivre" and of undermining the idea of "vivre ensemble," or "living together"). This coincidence in history is interpreted by some Muslims as a will of God, reinforcing their faith and letting them proudly claim their Muslim identity.

A Note on Terminology

Words for the Full-Face Veil

The garment that covers a woman's face goes by different names. The most common word, niqab, comes from the Arabic *an niqâb*, from the verb *naqaba*, which means to make a hole (for the eyes). In French, the term originally appeared in the *Le Robert* dictionary forty years ago, in 1982. There is also the hijab, the headscarf, which comes from the verb *hajaba*, "to cover"; this word appeared as "hidjab" in the *Petit Robert* in 1989, seven years after "niqab." Jilbab derives from the verb *jalaba*, "to be clothed"; this garment covers the entire body and can be accompanied by a niqab. Sitar comes from the Arabic word *satara*, which means "to hide" and refers to a variant of the niqab which involves an additional veil drawn over the eyes, resulting in total cover of the face.

The other recurring term for the facial veil is the burqa, from the Arabic *burqu'*, or "to hide one's face," which appeared in the *Petit Robert* in 1993. The Pakistani burqa, with its pastel colors, is almost identical to the Afghan *chadri*, with its net screen over the eyes, mandatory from 1996 to 2001 under Taliban rule, and again today since its return to power on August 15, 2021. After having been used to justify American military intervention in Afghanistan, the "burqa" was again the object of choice for proponents of the October 2010 law,[1] used to convince the French public of the necessity of a ban on the full-face veil. Although the burqa and the niqab are very different, the blue Afghan burqa still serves as the cover illustration for books and articles concerning the niqab, a conflation primarily used against French niqab wearers. (The term burqa does, however, refer to the black niqab worn in certain countries, including India.)

Haik refers to the traditional white veil worn in Algeria. It appeared in the French dictionary in 1830 (the year that Algeria came under French rule). Other face veils fall under local variations: the *m'laya* in Constantine (Algeria), the *ahouli* in the Mzeb region (southern Algeria), the *paranja* in Uzbekistan, the practice of *purdah* in Southeast Asia, and *battoulah* or *boregheh* for masks in the Persian Gulf region.

Figure 1. Conference at the Hotel Bristol, organized by Rachid Nekkaz, 2011. From left to right: a sitar, a niqab, and a niqab worn with dark glasses, three ways of hiding faces and hands.

Figure 2. A niqab and two sitars in the Basso Cambo neighborhood of Toulouse, 2012.

Words for Niqab Wearers

The correct Arabic term for a woman wearing the niqab is *moutanaqqiba*, or a woman who wears a garment with holes. This term, however, is not easily used in a French or English text. It is also problematic for our study, because it suggests that the women who wear the niqab in France come from outside of France or are at least Arabic speakers, which is rarely the case. The niqab, as it is studied here, is by and large adopted reactively among French women; it represents an act of borrowing, which permits wearers to forge a new identity for themselves. To use an Arabic term would, in a sense, falsify their reality.

The French language contains an interesting neologism: "niqabée," or woman wearing the niqab, which is the past participle of a second neologism, the verb "niqaber," or "to niqab," meaning to put on a niqab. The verb "to niqab" would thus be equivalent to the verb "to veil." The use of the reflexive form becomes "to niqab oneself," on the model of "to veil oneself." As an adjective, this construction yields a "niqabed woman," like a veiled woman. As a nominalized adjective, it is a "niqabée," just as one would say (in English) a retiree or a divorcée.[2] This construction, a woman who wears a niqab/niqab wearer/niqabée has the advantage of suggesting a voluntary action: a man wearing a helmet, a helmeted man. A woman who wears the niqab/niqab wearer/niqabée is the best solution here, even if it is not without problems of its own, reducing the woman in the niqab to her clothing alone, even though certain women wear it only occasionally. It makes sense too, though, with respect to their position: women who voluntarily claim the niqab might therefore be defined by the object of their claim.

Mahomet, Mohamed, or Muhammad

Faced with the multiple transcriptions of the prophet of Islam's name, I have followed the American historian John Tolan, who distinguishes the historical figure he describes as Muhammad from the character who has existed in the European imagination since the crusades, written as Mahomet.[3] As for the word prophet, it is not capitalized except when it is used by itself, the Prophet, and not when it is used as a common noun. Here we will refer to the prophet of Islam or the prophet Muhammad. We will also use Mohamed or Mohammed for individuals who are so named.

THE NIQAB IN FRANCE

PART I

Introduction

In France, the beginning of the twenty-first century was marked by the emergence of young Muslim men and women who publicly demonstrate their religious identity by assuming "Islamic" dress. The full veil appeared in the country, in a marginal way, during the years between 2005 and 2010, in the context of the stigmatization of the headscarf, especially in schools, which has now lasted for over two decades. The first public debate in the media over the veil, referred to in France as the *affaire du foulard* [headscarf controversy], occurred in September of 1989, when three middle-school students refused to remove their headscarves in class. This act led to their temporary expulsion and, fifteen years later, to the March 15, 2004 vote prohibiting the display of any religious symbols in schools.

The primary interest of this book is the full veil known as the niqab. The niqab became a specific object of controversy in France in June of 2009, following the establishment of a National Assembly commission that aimed to ban facial coverings in public spaces.[1] The study contained a representational bias: a single niqab wearer was considered for it, the mediagenic Kenza Drider.* Starting that summer, the press swarmed to cover the issue of the full-face veil, soliciting citizens across the board, with no prior knowledge of the subject, to voice their positions publicly and angrily. Male and female politicians alike invoked the niqab as a symbol of inequality between the sexes in Islam, accusing women who wear the niqab of disregarding both the rules of social convention and the norms that define "civilized" behavior. In full public view, a collective myth was erected around the niqab. This myth combines the colonial cliché of the Orientalized woman with a vision of France's "civilizing mission." In general, niqab wearers are seen to be deluded and in need of liberation from subjugation to men (read: unveiling). A universalist, feminist discourse assumes it is acting for their good, even against their will. At the same time, rumors around the niqab swirled, even to the point of suggesting that women were paid to wear the niqab by shadowy ambassadors from Muslim countries, in order to work toward an Islamic conquest of Europe. The issue of the veil still feeds into various conspiracy theories, reprised by emergent European populisms today, and its negative image is amplified, associated with Westerners who travel to join jihadist fighters in Syria and Iraq.

And yet, at the time the June 2009 French National Assembly commission was formed, niqab wearers made up a minuscule percentage of Muslim women in France. Their total number was estimated to be between 350 and 2,000 individuals, or less than .05% of French Muslim women and less than .003% of the French population. Despite this numerical insignificance, however, a law outlawing the niqab in France was passed on October 11, 2010, as part of a ban on all public face coverings. This law went into effect six months later, on April 11, 2011. After that date, women covering their faces were subject to a fine of 150 euros and mandatory citizenship classes. Even though wearing a facial covering is classified as a relatively minor offense in France,[2] the equivalent of using a cell phone while driving or driving in an emergency lane, a majority of French citizens saw these women as criminals (as the perpetrators of crimes, whereas they have only been fined), and some of them did not hesitate to use force on their own initiative to eliminate the infraction.

After France's ban on facial coverings in 2010 and Belgium's passage of a similar law in 2011, Bulgaria and Switzerland's Ticino canton followed suit in 2016, Austria and Quebec in 2017, and the Netherlands, Denmark, and the Swiss canton of St. Gallen in 2018. The whole of Switzerland passed the anti-burqa initiative (by a narrow majority) in a popular referendum in March 2021. These various laws are less restrictive than French law, and some of them apply only to public establishments. Although it is no longer possible to claim that opposition to the Muslim veil is linked solely to France's colonial past, many former French colonies took similar coercive action against the full-face veil, showing a form of allegiance to their former power. In 2015, five African countries banned its wearing: Chad, Cameroon, Gabon, Niger, and Senegal. In 2017, it was Morocco's turn to prohibit the fabrication and sale of the niqab. Algeria also banned the niqab that year for teachers and students, and then, in 2018, for civil servants. In Tunisia, as of July 2019, public institutions are no longer accessible to women wearing a facial veil.

And yet on the eve of the 2010 French vote, Amnesty International denounced France as particularly intolerant of visible manifestations of Islamic identity[3] (although the law was upheld by the European Court of Human

Rights on July 1, 2014). In October of 2018, the United Nations Committee for Human Rights criticized France for its law banning the niqab, which was described as too radical a measure.[4]

This French law had a paradoxical effect: it led to an increase in the number of niqab wearers. Before the ban, the full veil was generally an individual choice, involving only its wearers. It was simply a spiritual step, inspired by models of piety such as those disseminated, for example, on the Internet. The 2009 controversy described earlier, surrounding the so-called "burqa," led to the emulation of those targeted; it was followed by the 2010 ban, which rendered the niqab even more appealing to some. As society came to oppose the full-face veil, increasing numbers of women claimed the right to wear it.

The 2010 ban gave rise to a new concept: the "protest niqab." The passage of the law in France attracted new partisans of full-face coverings and led to the radicalization of some women. The Islamic State's rise to power in Syria and Iraq led, for a small minority of French Muslims, to belief in a new era of a fantasy caliphate. For some women, the Islamic State incarnated an ideal country, a place of *hegira* (the emigration to a Muslim country encouraged by Islam). Following the ban to which they were subject at home, some women have joined the jihad as a form of revenge. Isolated in France, they would unite in Syria.

The period of study that culminated in this book began in the fall of 2008 and continued for more than ten years. During this time, I was able to observe the phenomenon as it unfolded and to take account of the remarkable evolution of facial coverings in France, up to the point of their near disappearance at present. I happened upon a subject that is contemporary. At the moment of the October 2010 law's passage, it was impossible to imagine French women leaving for war-torn countries, and still less to imagine that they would justify their jihadist engagement by invoking the French law banning the full-face veil.

Today we are witnessing the niqab's decline. Some women who formerly wore the niqab—a small but significant number of this group—have mounted a critique of the full-face veil, decrying the abuse of power on the part of Salafi sheikhs and the system into which they were indoctrinated. Some of them have even abandoned the practice of Islam. Across more than a decade, I have followed the course of the full-face veil's evolution, tracking it from a rare phenomenon through its exponential spread due to the 2010 law, studying its instrumentalization by women who wore it as a sign of opposition, and finally witnessing its increasing scarcity, albeit with occasional, sporadic resurgences.

This research was carried out in the suburbs of Paris, primarily in the Seine-Saint-Denis region, as well as around Toulouse, and in Lille and its surroundings. My area of study occasionally extended as far as London, Birmingham, and Brussels. I also studied comparative facial covering practices at Darul

Uloom Deoband, the Islamic university and religious center of the Indian state of Uttar Pradesh, as well as in Qatar, and in post-revolutionary Tunisia, which saw the spread of full-face veiling after the uprising of January 14, 2011.

My sample of Muslim women who wear the niqab was constituted in a fairly aleatory manner, through encounters with niqab wearers in the street, in Salafi mosques, in housing developments and working-class neighborhoods, and in mass gatherings such as the annual Muslim meeting celebrated in Le Bourget or on the Rue Jean-Pierre Timbaud in Paris's 11th arrondissement, where Islamic establishments include both bookstores and clothing stores; this busy street is where the Paris region's Muslim population comes to shop.[5] Finally, I also made contact with the various groups established to protect the rights of niqab wearers ("Amazons for Freedom" ["Amazones de la liberté"], and "Citizens for Freedom" ["Citoyennes de la liberté"]), after the law was passed.

The majority of woman wearing the full-face veil with whom I spoke anticipated confrontation regarding the garment, especially in moments in which the niqab became the object of heightened media attention. In some early encounters, they cited religious discourse to justify facial coverings, often giving rote arguments: "The full veil is a duty; the Quran says so and I wear it to obey God." Often, they sought to portray themselves as the image of the obedient and pious Muslim woman using formulaic language. These women were persuaded that their actions were purely religious. But these kinds of explanations are too stereotypical to shed any light on actual personalities. Other factors—more prosaic ones—were also part of their motivation for wearing the veil. To understand the niqab's attraction requires more intimacy than a cursory interview can provide, and to further my study, I needed access to these women's interior universes. Indeed, after I spent whole days with them, some women ultimately revealed motives of which they themselves had not always been conscious. As our meetings continued, a majority of these women came to seem quite different than they had appeared at first glance. For this reason, my research needed to take place over time, following the women as deeply as possible into their private lives, even up to the point at which some of them opted to disappear, changing telephone numbers and contact information. I met over 200 niqab wearers and conducted, with some of them, hundreds of interviews, carried out primarily in their homes. Always, I kept their subjectivity and individuality at the forefront; I became a witness to their lives and to the exclusion to which they were subject. I listened to those affected explain their choices without the filters of the Internet or social media. I received their confidences about their families and their emotional attachments, listening attentively to their still-raw childhood injuries, their silences, and the trials that led them to the steps that seemed so radical in the eyes the general populace.

A Muslim woman wearing a full veil is the object of stereotypes buried so deep in the French collective unconscious that it is risky even to question them. In general, veiled women are judged to be subjugated and subordinate to masculine pressure. Failing to convince audiences of the contrary, I decided, starting at the end of 2009, to film our exchanges. The results exceeded even my own expectations. A substantial number of niqab wearers were interested in taking part in the proceedings, hoping to find a way to be heard and seen through my filming. This video material would lead to eight documentaries (four of them centered in France), all of which would serve to invite the viewer into these women's personalities.[6]

In my filming, I was inspired by the French anthropologist Jean Rouch's practice of *cinéma vérité*, or footage shot spontaneously and simply, sacrificing the image's aesthetic quality for a sense of authenticity and an interactive relationship with the filmed subject. Working in this tradition, I filmed without any disturbances from external technicians and with synchronous sound, direct and unaltered. In the vein of this direct cinema technique, I also chose to undertake the editing myself.

Quotations from women featured in this book are taken from my four documentaries on the phenomenon in France: *Sous la burqa [Beneath the Burqa]* (2010); *Niqab Hors-la-loi [Outlaw Niqab]* (2012); *Émilie König vs Ummu Tawwab* (2016); and *Voile interdit [Forbidden Veil]* (2017), as well as from unfilmed and informal exchanges. First names followed by an asterisk are the subject of detailed portraits found later in this book's second part. I have kept the last names of women who became publicly known in France through media attention, including Kenza Drider,* Hind Ahmas,* Émilie König,* and Naïma S.* I replaced other names with pseudonyms, but I have not kept to Salafi convention. In general, Salafi women refer to themselves by the name of their child after the word Oum ("mother," in Arabic), for example, Oum Zainab (Zainab's mother). They are defined through maternity even if they have no children.[7] Keeping these names would have led to a profusion of the word "Oum" and confusion for the reader.

This book runs the risk of giving offense to at least two groups of people. First, Salafi Muslims, for the revelations it contains about women who wear the niqab, whose status as the image of piety is seriously undermined; and second, opponents of the veil who, conditioned by the most cliché of clichés, refuse to let the subjects at the origin of their obsessions express themselves.

My work has no theological pretensions. Its goal is not to determine whether the niqab is or is not prescribed in Islamic jurisprudence, nor is it to revisit controversy around the hijab. It seems to me inappropriate to declare that the veil or the niqab are not "Quranic," bypassing centuries of exegesis, as certain contemporary thinkers do. I have absolutely no intention of interpreting the Quran or of discussing any of its disputed passages.

In what follows, I study a set of women who think of the niqab as a religious recommendation or obligation—the two tendencies coexist. Instead of determining the doctrinal status of their belief, my intention is to understand why they keep to this injunction, as well as the benefits that they gain from it. I record their feelings while being careful not to comment at all on their decision to wear the full veil or take it off.

I approach the women who appear in this book as autonomous subjects, with control over their own lives and the ability to speak about them. The woman wearing the niqab is the subject, and the niqab is the object. But for many French citizens, the relationship is inverted: the niqab is the topical subject, and the woman who wears it reduced to the level of an object, with neither her own will nor the capacity of speech. Women who wear the niqab, however, are of course subjects in their own right with the capacity for introspection, self-analysis, and reflexivity.

Finally, let us note that this is a study of women wearing the niqab and not the jihadist women with whom they are often conflated. It is true that the latter group generally wears the niqab, but not always—take, for example, Inès Madani, age nineteen, and Ornella Gillgmann, age twenty-nine, responsible for the attempted gas cylinder attack in front of Notre Dame Cathedral in Paris on the night of September 3–4, 2016. Nevertheless, I witnessed some women turn toward jihadist ideology, including Émilie König* and Saliha,* and have included others who renounced it from the beginning but remained sympathetic to the cause of armed jihad, such as Naïma S.,* arrested while in possession of a knife at the Austerlitz train station on January 6, 2020.

The Niqab and Re-Islamization Movements

Religious practices, in general, fall into two sorts: religious traditions inherited from parents, in which individuals have been raised in a tradition from childhood and which benefit from official recognition, and those that are re-invented, adapted for a specific population, and reconnected a posteriori to constructed origins.

In France, Muslim believers can also be divided into two groups according to this pattern: traditional Muslims (new immigrants and their children, educated in religion by their parents), and Muslims by conversion or re-Islamization (from assimilated families) who returned to the religion as adolescents or young adults. These individuals come to religion in a way similar to "born-again Christians" who speak of their religion as a "reconversion." With the use of the term "conversion" to describe Muslims in a process of re-Islamization, we can thus oppose an "original Islam" to an "Islam of converts."

The full-face veil has spread internationally via Islamic missionary trends, or Islamic revival movements, referred to as "re-Islamization." These trends are not so much a return to the past, as they claim to be, as the contemporary manifestation of an individualist religiosity. First appearing in the nineteenth and early twentieth centuries, they were developed over the course of the previous century and continue to evolve today. They stem from modernity and gave birth to contemporary attitudes valuing an Islam that is made visible by clothing and manifest piety, as well as a strict diet (only products labeled strictly halal). This book addresses two main movements in this vein: Tablighi Jamaat and Salafism (as well as Takfirism, a version of Salafism). These two groups appeared relatively recently and have seen an expansion in France across the past fifty years. Both groups have a transnational impact; their common ground is a fight against *bid'ah*, or "blameworthy innovation," that encourages a return to an idealized Islamic origin presented as "authentic." Such literalism explains the terms "fundamentalist" or "neo-fundamentalist" that are linked to these identities.

Tablighi Jamaat

The Tablighi Jamaat is a missionary re-Islamization movement founded on the Indian sub-continent in 1927, originating from the Muslim reform promoted by the school of Darul Uloom Deoband in northern India's Uttar Pradesh. Its objective is to work toward *dawah* (call), the act of proselytizing toward non-practicing Muslims with a set program and strict framework. The Tablighi Jamaat is seen as the major transnational Muslim movement and boasts activity in 135 countries across the globe. Its secrecy, however, means that the orientation is largely unknown, despite its numbers. The movement is founded on obedience to a leader (*ameer*).

Tablighi women practicing *dawah* teach other women the principles of Islam according to the movement's doxa, encouraging them to engage in missionary activity. These women take on new responsibilities and functions almost identical to those of men. The American historian Barbara Metcalf has studied Tablighi women;[8] she rebuts conceptions that the re-Islamization process entails a regression for women and has shown how their religious engagement creates a break with their quotidian reality and upends the relationship between the sexes. Through activities such as teaching, canvassing, and discussing the merits of religion, Tablighi women take on a new form of sociability and roles that were traditionally reserved for men and therefore inaccessible to them.

Indeed, women's participation was seen as indispensable by the movement's founders as a way of promoting engagement among men. Involving wives, rather than leaving them in the shadows, was part of a strategy to increase the effectiveness of *dawah*. Thanks to female engagement, the Tablighi Jamaat enters into the private family sphere: women push their husbands to leave on *khurūj* (missionary travel in order to proselytize). They accept their husband's negligence of family affairs, supporting him even in a society quick to criticize a man seen as fleeing family obligations. They also pass on *dawah* to their children.

The Tablighi Jamaat also offers its female adherents the charge of traveling worldwide through *khurūj*, in accordance with a very codified protocol. During missionary voyages, undertaken in couples, the niqab is required. I have often heard Tablighi women excited to enumerate the countries to which they and their spouses have been sent for *dawah*. Their abnegation of the world, represented by the wearing of the niqab, valorizes them in Tablighi microsociety. By the distinction it confers, the niqab gives its wearers a sense of social elevation. They see themselves as the elect: "We must thank Allah for having chosen us from among women" is a formula that recurs frequently at the beginning of meetings. In addition, for Tablighi women, donning the niqab and black gloves can signal to the outside world that they are offered the luxury of not working in order to devote themselves entirely to *dawah*, leaving on *khurūj* to travel across the globe.

The Tablighi Jamaat established itself in France during the 1970s, alongside a generation of men arriving from other countries to work in factories without any social structure. These new arrivals benefited from the movement's networks of solidarity. Although the Tablighi Jamaat has prospered in the first influx of migrants, this form of religion is (relatively) infrequently transferred to children born in France, who no longer need the networks sought out by their fathers who arrived alone. The full-face veil thus appeared only rarely before the arrival of the neo-Salafi who have rendered it more common since 2005.

Salafism

Unlike Tablighi, Salafism has no hierarchical system. It is born out of a strain of theological thinking that is linked to the Hanbali tradition followed in Saudi Arabia, by way of Ibn Taymiyyah (1263–1328) and Muhammad Ibn Abd al-Wahhab (1703–1729). The Salafi rarely refer to themselves as such, describing themselves instead as following the *Salafi Manhaj*, or the way of the *salaf*, the pious ancestors, three generations of Muhammad's companions. To "follow *manhaj*"[9] is a widely used expression for introducing oneself as Salafi without using the term. The women of *manhaj* make reference to Saudi Arabian sheikhs, including Abd al-Aziz ibn Abd Abdullah ibn Baaz (1912–1999), Muhammad ibn al-Uthaymin (1929–2001), Rabee al-Madkhali (1931–), Salih al-Fawzan (1933–), and the traditionalist al-Albani, a Hadith specialist (1914–1999).

Whereas Tablighi missionaries tend to use more basic means of communication (telephone, going door-to-door), Salafism has adapted to modernity and its new technologies. The figures who help create a given Salafi individual's religious and social milieu rarely meet physically. Modern Salafi replaces group *dawah* with virtual connections. Its members have no need for courses; they get their information from the Internet and tend to develop their viewpoints without the intermediation of an apprenticeship under any master.

It is customary to distinguish between pietist Salafi, who practice *jihad al-akhbar*, or major jihad, an effort on oneself, and jihadists who promote *jihadal-asghar*, minor jihad, which is synonymous with armed combat. It must be noted that jihadist niqab wearers are rare. On the whole, the Salafi movement remains non-violent, apolitical, and pacifist. The majority of niqab wearers are against jihadism. Sabine, for instance, is a convert to Islam, born in 1980 to parents of Spanish origin. One of the first women to wear the niqab, she has done so since 2004. In her words:

> *Those who carry out massacres shouldn't be called Salafi. ISIS is a form of terrorism that brings shame to all Muslims. We are in danger because of them. That's not what Islam is: we don't kill innocent people. Those acts aren't part of the Prophet's tradition. The Prophet was insulted a lot throughout his lifetime but he forbade reacting. He was always forgiving and showed good character. But what's happening now is disastrous.*

Tablighi Jamaat and Salafism are based less on deep theological understanding than on a rigorous religious practice. The members of these groups acquire a new identity thanks to the characteristic garments that let them express their convictions publicly. Men seek to imitate the behavior of Mohammed and his companions as recorded in the Hadiths, collections of the Prophet's words and acts. For men, this entails wearing a *qamis* (long shirt), *kopiah* (cap), and beard.

The models to imitate for women are the Prophet's wives, who, according to tradition, wore the niqab. Louisa is twenty-one years old and a convert to Islam. She is in her first year of studying Arabic at university and explains her desire to resemble this mythologized model, recalling the doxa of imitating the pious *salaf*:

> *Our role as Muslims is to look like the Prophet and the pious forerunners [salaf] who accompanied him. So for men, the* sunna *for being like them*

is the beard and for women it's the veil or the sitar. All the Prophet's wives covered their faces—all of them! And all of the companions' wives wore them.

The full-face veil is promoted by both schools. These garments, supposedly identical to those worn in the Prophet's time, entail a performative dimension: they announce the piety and the obedience of those who wear them. In the words of Rosezalina, a devout Malaysian Tablighi: "People in the Tablighi Jamaat show their faith through their clothing." The Salafi also use these codes of self-presentation as a way of asserting themselves in modern society.

The two groups are both similar—each advocates a return to fundamentals and an imitation of religious models—and in competition, rivals in the market of Islamic revival. Both groups promote a degree of showiness among members dressed to exhibit their faith through their clothing, although differences include features such as the length of the *qamis* and the absence of a *serban* (turban) among Salafi men. Both groups champion conduct that runs counter to the norms of Western society. Factors contributing to the rise of each group include their rejection of Western values and "looser" morals, as well as of traditions from countries of origin, giving younger adherents a sense of power over older generations, including their parents. Women who wear the niqab share the characteristic of having claimed their religious identity a posteriori, not from family heritage.

Membership in each group tends to correspond to types: Tablighi women are often married women who identify as virtuous and agree to enter into the movement's strict framework. Salafism attracts independent, single, or divorced women, women whose lifestyles might lead them to prefer virtual support rather than judgment from a group in which each woman is responsible for the others. For most modern women, it is difficult to accept the intrusion into private life prescribed by the Tablighi Jamaat—especially difficult for women who seek freedom from social control.

Tablighi and Salafi women also tend to hold different relationships to the niqab. For the Salafi, where belonging depends on individual will, rather than hierarchical control, the niqab becomes a tool for self-expression, for faith made visible in public spaces. Salafi women tend to give very personal explanations for their approach. For the Tablighi, on the other hand, the niqab represents a strict clothing norm employed to prevent proximity with the other sex that could lead to illicit relations. Out of respect for the state, a fundamental Tablighi principle, adherents to this movement in France have, for the most part, chosen to bare their faces in accordance with the law. In Salafism, the niqab lets a woman go out alone without the presence of a *mahram* (a husband or close family member with whom marriage is forbidden) or two other women. Such company, however, is still expressly mandated by the Tablighi Jamaat—too strict a condition for the majority of single or divorced niqab wearers without a father or brother to serve a *mahram* for them. Salafi women can go out as they wish, independently. They are not obligated to obey any individual person, except perhaps for a virtual sheikh who gives Internet advice and whom each member chooses to follow, or not. Several women in our study were involved with the Tablighi Jamaat before choosing Salafism, including Hanane* and Claire.*

Forsane Alizza and Takfiri

Forsane Alizza (Knights of Pride) is a small, militant, French group founded in 2010 and banned by French Interior Minister Claude Guéant on March 1, 2012. The group was founded by Mohamed Achamlane, from the French city of Nantes, who took the nickname Abou Hamza after formerly using the childish nickname Cortex.[10] Its rise, militancy, and combative rhetoric can be linked to the ban's legislation and the excessive police control and brutality it entailed for women who wear the niqab. Achamlane contacted a niqab wearer named Sophie* after she was assaulted in a zoo, using her story, even against her wishes, to escalate conflict. The case of Hind Ahmas* represents a similar situation; she was arrested and handcuffed in Aulnay-sous-Bois on July 31, 2011. After seeing amateur footage posted on YouTube the evening of the event, Achamlane made contact with her and launched a call for a rally. The rally took place a week later, on August 6, 2011, in a public square in Aulnay-sous-Bois; I was present to film it.[11] More than one hundred men were present, while Hind kept her distance along with another niqab wearer, Alexia.* Achamlane spoke to his audience using a megaphone:

> *We are going to show you what we think of this disgusting, destructive law that has loosed the real Fascists. They're laughing at us, the bluebloods, the purebred dogs.*[12] *Here's what I do with their Penal Code, the code that includes no respect at all for us. I tread on it. I tread on it like they've trodden on the Quran.*

Achamlane then held a new copy of the penal code up to the crowd, opened it, placed it on the ground, poured gasoline over it, and set it on fire, a dramatic action intended to be memorable. The rally provided an occasion for men wearing *qamis*, and generally excluded from the society in which they were living, to overturn their humiliation. For them, it was an occasion to demonstrate their integrity, purity, goodness, and commitment to the honor of their religious sisters, assuming a posture of devotion to the women who were victims of discrimination, the majority of whom were single mothers awaiting "brothers" to come to their defense.

Often wrongly identified as jihadist, Forsane Alizza's thinking resembles what is known as Takfiri ideology. Takfirism rejects any allegiance to *taghut*, or "that which is worshipped other than Allah," a phrase used to refer to the state, its justice, and its institutions. Takfirism claims the right to excommunicate Muslims who do not adhere to its ideology, although it does not call for them to be killed. Alexia,* at the time an active member of Forsane Alizza and a committed Takfiri, explains:

> *We're not at all like kamikaze or terrorists; for us, it's forbidden to kill the innocent. But we must give up* taghut, *the laws and all the administration. We cannot get married at town halls. When we practice* takfir, *which means calling people infidels when they deserve it, we don't aim at Muslims but at true infidels, those who truly are* kufar *[disbelievers] with established proof. A person known for not praying or keeping Ramadan is an infidel. Even a Muslim who does pray falls into* shirk *[idolatry] by going to vote. A good example is Chalhgoumi.*[13] *A few years ago, he defended women wearing the niqab and then he changed sides. He's a hypocritical idiot and so is Dalil Boubakeur.*[14] *These two want us to believe that they represent Islam in France while in fact they're in line with the enemy. The Muslim scholars made Chalghoumi into an infidel. The Arab leaders are infidels! For us, we call them* talafi, *or pseudo-Salafi because they accept all deviances in Islam. But you have to be careful, it's tricky to practice* takfir *without knowing what the scholars say. I'm staying out of it because it might come back against me if I practice* takfir *wrongly.*

Takfiri disavow Saudi Salafi sheiks such as ibn Baaz, al-Uthaymin, and al-Albani, accusing them of having links to *taghut*, or Saudi power, and calling them (ironically) the "palace scholars." Alexia,* uncompromising, judges them based on their relationship to the niqab:

> *Sheikh Albani is a* murji *[anti-literalist], too lax religiously. It's not acceptable. The Saudi Arabian scholars issue fatwas that are totally nonsensical. I only like al-Uthaymin. He was the one who made the niqab make sense to me, through his videos and his texts translated into French. He forbids women to take off the niqab in France. He says that "the obligation for a woman to be covered head to foot is unanimous," and I agree completely.*

Among the women of Forsane Alizza, a majority are converts, such as Christy (Mohamed Achamlane's wife), Peggy, Laurene, and Éva, the four female names included on the list of active members who had their bank accounts frozen after the group was banned in 2012. Over the course of my study, I spent time with three niqab wearers who were members of Forsane Alizza: Alexia,* Saliha,* and Émilie König.*

Mohamed Achamlane was arrested at his home on March 30, 2012, charged with criminal conspiracy related to a terrorist group and possession of weapons. He was sentenced to nine years in prison in 2015 and was released on January 1, 2020.

The Sociology of Niqab Wearers

The Neo-Niqab

Today, the reclamation of the veil by Westernized, modern women has gone against the predictions of those who forecast its disappearance in tandem with the education of women. As the sociologist Nilufer Göle states:

> The reappearance of the veil is surprising and troubling, because it is a feature of religious traditions that were predicted to disappear with the impact of modernization. The phenomenon is interpreted by public opinion in both Western and Muslim countries as a sign of the failure of modernization's progress. The veil is even more surprising because it appears in modern spaces such as large urban areas and university campuses.[1]

It is an error to believe that the niqab is worn in Europe in a traditional manner. Like the veil, the niqab is a manifestation of modernization. It is linked to the abandonment of tradition, and it can be a way for certain women to assert themselves through difference—today, through visible Islam. In France, the niqab and the jilbab represent a tradition that has been reinvented without any link to the original cultures in which their wearing originated. Although the white haik was widespread across Northern Africa during the colonial period, incarnating resistance during the Algerian war, the full veil has practically disappeared in the countries of origin of those who have immigrated to France. Local versions of the face veil still exist in places, such as today's *ahouli*, worn in the Mzab region of Algeria, or the *sefsari* in Tunisia, but these have little in common with the transnational black neo-niqab that ties around the forehead.

The United Kingdom is exceptional in Europe: in the UK, the niqab is often worn by women from Pakistan, a country where the garment is customary in some regions. Both girls and their mothers wear it out of respect for familial tradition. Nevertheless, the UK has also seen the rise of the neo-niqab worn by modern women, second-generation immigrants (often of Somali origin), or converts.

In France, the neo-niqab is not worn by first-generation immigrants, but generally by French citizens born in French territories, educated for the most part in public schools. Those born in North Africa, or in sub-Saharan Africa, arrived very young. We could name at least one exception: Fazia Silmi, a Moroccan woman who saw her request for French citizenship refused in 2008 because of her full-face veil and "insufficient assimilation"—a development seen as the beginning of the controversy that arose in 2009. Nevertheless, this sort of profile is very rare.

The difference between the traditional veil and the actively reappropriated veil is particularly visible in French mosques: women from Muslim countries wearing more or less traditional clothing, often in several various colors, tend to occupy one side of the room, while on the other side are "re-Islamized" women uniformly wearing the jilbab, sometimes with a niqab in black or another dark color, with no personal accessories. The two groups, differentiated in this way, correspond schematically to the "older" and the "modern," but are not related to age or even generation, since young women educated in their countries of origin generally have no need to adopt Salafi apparel. Between the two groups of women, interactions are minimal or even nonexistent.

The neo-niqab is imbued with new significance: for the women who wear it, it represents the expression of certain demands, the sign of a religious identity that was repressed by their parents and is newly reclaimed. But we should not overestimate the religious element. For some women who wear the niqab, the exhibition of their faith through clothing is coupled with religious knowledge that is only cursory. Olivier Roy makes a similar claim about jihadist men:

> ... jihadis do not descend into violence after poring over sacred texts. They do not have the necessary religious culture—and, above all, care little about having one. They do not become radicals because they have misread the texts or because they have been manipulated. They are radicals because they choose to be, because only radicalism appeals to them.[2]

A similar ignorance can be observed in women who have just started wearing the niqab. In France, the majority of these women have little religious background except for a rudimentary Arabic vocabulary. They rarely know the literary Arabic that would allow them to read the Quran. If they come from North Africa, their language knowledge is often limited to their parents' dialects. Some niqab wearers learn verses of the Quran or Arabic invocations by heart with the aid of phonetic transcriptions. What is represented here is a new Francophone religiosity based on literature published in France by Muslim publishing houses, found primarily in Paris, Lyon, and Brussels. There is a commercial element to such work: specialized boutiques sell religious clothing and books, complete kits, so to speak, for assuming the full outfit of a new religious identity. The niqab has many meanings. It is worn and appropriated in different ways. Each woman who wears a niqab has her own history and a more or less fusional relationship with the garment.

French Niqab Wearers: An Overview

French women who have converted to Islam form a disproportionate majority of full-face veil wearers. An obvious classification would therefore be to divide niqab wearers into two groups: European converts, on the one hand, and women of Muslim origin, on the other. But this distinction would not be particularly helpful: the latter group also consider themselves converts, since they come from families who have repressed or minimized their religious heritage. The stories from both groups of women who have chosen to wear the niqab are similar, involving a quest for a religiosity that they see as lacking in their upbringing. This study, thus, does not separate European converts and those of Muslim origin into two separate groups, even if we take pains to mention the detail. Let us begin by laying out the most common and most noticeable facts about niqab wearers in France and Belgium.

Family Situation

A general sketch of niqab-wearing women highlights similarities that often occur in family environments. The women who call themselves *manhaj Salafi* (on the model of the Prophet) differ from their male counterparts; they often come from more affluent, less densely populated areas rather than from suburban housing developments. They describe their childhood houses with yards and often a dog—an idealized version of the French petite bourgeoisie.

The father figure has often been problematic in their upbringing, tending to be simultaneously missing or cruel, as well as idealized. The jihadist Émilie König,* for example, who was the object of much media attention in France, was abandoned by her father, although he did acknowledge her and although she always professes her love for him. Other women, such as Naïma S.,* describe growing up with tyrannical fathers remembered for physical violence or sexual abuse; often this situation ends in the parents' divorce. The father as authority figure is often also missing from family life. Coupled with the father's abdication, the mother is often tyrannical toward her daughter, codependent and overbearing. For adolescent or post-adolescent girls and women, the niqab can serve as a break from their parents, even if this damages the family reputation. Wearing the niqab can be seen as a way to inflict a symbolic punishment on family, and especially on the simultaneously missing and authoritarian father figure.

Several of the women in my study are the daughters of public figures. Émilie König's* father was a police officer. Similarly, Claire's* father was a police commissioner; he received the official violation notice for his daughter's face covering while at home when she was still a minor. Stéphanie's* father was an employee at the police headquarters when he discovered his daughter's conversion to Islam through a general information communication. We find other instances of figures of authority who are close to niqab wearers: a husband in the military, for Sandra; or a mother who was the president of an anti-radicalization organization in Brussels, for Shamsou, whose search for self-affirmation arose from a longstanding struggle with her mother, who was organizing public events in the Belgian capital at the moment Shamsou chose to appear for the first time wearing the niqab. I first met her at a similar conference on jihadism, in 2016.

Other women portray their parents as having accepted their choice even though it goes "against their principles," most likely considering it a temporary phase. Still, here, mother figures tend to be overrepresented. Filmed at a demonstration by niqab wearers in Paris's Place de la République in 2010, nine months before the ban was passed, Louisa (twenty-one years old at the time) stated:

> *My mother is a feminist, 200%. My parents have pretty high positions in society: they're architects. They're cultured and they've traveled everywhere, they know lots of politicians. At first they didn't really understand. But my parents know that I make my own choices, for myself, and they know that I'm a strong person and I do what I want. For them, what's important is that I'm happy. I'm happy like this.*

Deficient Religious Education

If fathers are often absent in the upbringings of French niqab wearers, so too is religion. One of the constants observed among the converted niqab wearers in my sample is their a-religious—even anti-religious—family background. The converts sometimes recount having been hindered in their quest for spirituality by their parents. As Louisa describes:

> My parents are atheist: they don't believe in God. I had no religious education whatsoever. I read the Quran then after I converted, and then I started praying very quietly, and then one thing led to another and here we are with me wearing the niqab.

Alexia,* who converted to Islam at seventeen years old, remembers having been forced to pray in secret:

> Spirituality was forbidden for my whole childhood. My parents were atheists. I had to hide to pray—I was always attracted to religion. They were shocked by my conversion to Islam.

Converts who choose to wear the full veil often recount parental Islamophobia. They describe the shock produced for their friends and family by their decision to wear the niqab. We might interpret this radical clothing choice as revenge against parents perceived as unworthy and despotic. It also serves as a means of emancipation, a pretext for leaving the family home.

European converts to Islam are not the only women seeking a religious identity that had not been part of their heritage. Women from families originally from North Africa also decide to wear the niqab. The mothers of such women are generally not veiled or adopt the veil late in life (often after their daughters). Here too, the reclamation of a visible Islamic identity might be understood as resentment toward parents who repressed their religious identities as a way to complete their assimilation into French society.

Malika El Aroud, the wife of Dahmane Abd el-Sattar, the suicide bomber who assassinated the Afghan commander Massoud on September 9, 2001, was one of the first French proponents of the full-face veil. In her book, she recounts her discovery of the religious roots that were denied her by her parents:

> This North African delinquency responds to the suffering that follows the feeling of identity loss on the part of the Moroccan immigrant's parents, and of which I was a victim myself but against which I reacted in the same way as my husband, although we hadn't yet met. By learning my culture of origin for the first time, the Muslim religion so rich and so fair, I too, one day during Ramadan, I too was touched by the grace of Islam.[3]

The reproach of progenitors' educational shortcomings recurs often in remarks by niqab-wearing women of Muslim origin, as well as in those of converts. Imen, from Toulouse, talks about wearing the niqab after the law's passage. Originally from a non-practicing family, she affirms that she was convinced to begin wearing the niqab by her father's hostile reaction to it. These women often express regret at having to discover their religion alone. Shamsou, for instance, eighteen years old and born in Brussels to Moroccan parents, says:

> No one steered me towards Islam. No one told me to wear the veil. I had to do all my own research, repent for myself—I do it for myself and for Allah, not for my parents.

Parental religious shortcomings also feature in reproaches by Salafi men. Sandrine Moulères, for instance, describes her husband, Lies Hebbaj:

> He came to France from Algeria in 1977, when he was only two years old. He grew up in a non-practicing Muslim family that was able to find its place in French society. Lies, though, became interested on his own in Islam during high school. He was already religious but little by little felt the need to practice his faith with more rigor and more fervor, although this did not keep him from continuing his studies in economics and social sciences at the university level.[4]

The children of assimilated North Africans often seek a strong identity to counterbalance what has been lost in generational transmission. As Olivier Roy writes, modern fundamentalisms do not represent the reactivation of the religious aspects of any "traditional" culture, but are, on the contrary, part of a process of deculturation.[5]

Unlike the veiled women of religious tradition, women who wear the niqab are not "determined" by their social milieu into choosing Salafi Islam. On the contrary: their friends and families oppose it. Instead, they consciously question their education and their own cultures. The paradox of niqab wearing in France is that it evokes the idea of free choice, exaggerated into an individualism that seeks to be free from any and all external limitation, while nevertheless imposing a voluntary constraint on the body itself.

Absence of Masculine Coercion

In my first documentary on the niqab in France, *Sous la burqa* (2010), I dedicated a part of my work to niqab wearers who made their autonomy from men visible. This is one of the points that runs most contrary to popular intuition. Here I reproduce some remarks from Muslim women who wear the niqab:

SAFIYA (CONVERT): *No one forced me. I've never had a woman wearing the niqab tell me that they forced her. Because if there's a woman who's forced, I think there are lots of organizations for her to help defend herself. We live in a country where we're free in every sense of the term.*

ASMA (MUSLIM ORIGINS): *Personally, I've never met women who submit to their husbands, fathers, brothers, or anyone else. Instead, it's always them—they fight with their family to be able to wear it. It's the opposite of what people think.*

KARIMA (MUSLIM ORIGINS): *When I got married, I'd already been wearing it for quite a few years. My husband wasn't the one who came to talk to me about it. No, my husband has never interfered with how I dress, either at home or outside.*

LOUISA (CONVERT): *Personally, I was married and I was the one who wanted a divorce because my husband wasn't active enough in his religion. For me, we weren't spiritually compatible. They told me I was wearing it because I was submissive. I'm not married anymore so now they can't say it's my husband who forced me to wear it. A man who forces his wife to wear something knows that his act will be rejected by God because the intention has to be for God, always. That means that if a woman wears the niqab or the veil for her husband, her act will have no value in God's eyes. I feel better like this, I feel comfortable in my life like this. I've never felt any pressure.*

The activist Lila,* who ran a telephone hotline out of her home through her organization, "Amazons for Freedom," established to help women who were fined for their full veils, is familiar with the community of niqab wearers. In 2012, she summarized a first year of calls, highlighting the absence of any external pressure faced by these women in France:

> *I reiterate often that the single merit of the law is that it's proven that no woman has been or is forced. In fact, since my group was founded in April 2011, we have received zero calls from women forced by their husband or by a third party. All the women who have called the hotline are women who wear the full veil of their own volition and who desire it in their heart and who are ready to do anything to keep wearing it, even against their husband's wishes.*

In March 2017, Hind Ahmas* expresses her incredulity at the hypothesis of pressure from men:

> *No woman can say she's forced by her husband into wearing the niqab. The brothers who want a woman who wears the niqab have lots of women*

to choose from. They're not going to go for a woman wearing just a veil to convince her to cover her face—it just doesn't make sense. It's just another way of making people believe we're just submissive women without any sense.

Sandrine Moulères became one of the first women to be the object of media fascination when she was pulled over while driving and fined in April of 2010, before the law had, in fact, been passed (her fine would later be annulled). In her book, published in Paris, she recounts her version of the facts.[6] Her fine led to another media scandal involving her husband, Lies Hebbaj, arrested for polygamy and benefit fraud, and later for rape. All these charges were dismissed in 2013. Sandrine Moulères proved to be a commandeering woman, the "matron" for her husband's wives.

I myself met no women who were pressured into wearing the niqab, and I can conclude that the stereotype of the woman wearing the niqab due to masculine pressure is an imaginary construction that, in reality, does not exist— or at least is so rare that it does not merit discussion. This is further evidenced by the fact that, to the best of my knowledge, no man has been sentenced for "forced hiding of the face," even though the law mandates a year in prison and a fine of 30,000 euros (doubled in the case of a minor) for any person who forces another to "cover their face because of their gender"[7]—proof that male coercion has yet to be demonstrated.

I was, however, contacted by email and by telephone by two women following the publication of one of my articles.[8] Both of them, especially Lina,* spoke of wearing the niqab and complained to me of unhealthy relationships with their husbands, accusing the men of profiting from the limitation of their movements, in order to subject them to psychological torture. Because of the law, they found themselves stuck at home out of fear of being arrested or assaulted. Another niqab wearer in my study, Naïma S.,* also experienced abuse by her husband, who used social pressure in a form of blackmail. But this type of dependent relationship is also found in other contexts that bear no relation to Islam or the niqab. Instead of "liberating" these women, the law rendered them even more vulnerable, since they no longer had access to public spaces and associations that fight domestic violence.

The Niqab and Feminine Beauty Standards

Multiple women included in this study began work as beauticians fairly young, attracted by the beautification of the body. These women recount having cherished dreams of working in the fashion and beauty industries, and often remember having been fascinated by the world of attraction and appearances. After the initial appeal, however, they often (quickly) become disenchanted by the thankless work, as is the case with Alexia,* working in a beauty store in Paris. In reality, the prestigious careers they hope for turn out to be quite the opposite.

For these women, Islam offers another path to fulfilling their desire for social recognition: a worldview in which aesthetics are illusory and beauty is interior. The Internet sheikhs make clear that the need for attractiveness is a sin. There is no need to seduce (except in the case of their husbands) in order to be happy. The solution is to adopt the model of a virtuous life, becoming chaste and reserving physical beauty, abandoning the world to disappear beneath the full veil, which represents the antithesis of a career in beauty. The move to hide the body represents a renunciation of the aesthetics of the body. The niqab, paradoxically, yields a feeling of freedom. Its wearers often feel liberated from the physical norms imposed by society and simultaneously fascinated by the aesthetic dimension of the full veil—the desire to be seen and distinguished is not effaced, but now it is put in service of what is considered a virtue.

Three Groups of Niqab Wearers

The most relevant classification I was able to draw from the phenomenon of the niqab in France was a differentiation of niqab wearers by age range, also linked to differing experiences with men.

The first group includes women between the ages of fifteen and twenty-two, although these ages are approximate and certain women already belong to the second group at age twenty. In general, this first group can be described as post-adolescent women who often live with their parents, frequently with their mothers alone. They have never been married and are "virgin" in terms of relationship experience. Often, they are in search of "true love." Through Salafi Islam, they find a way to emancipate themselves from their families, who they accuse of a life without any religious foundation, among other things. They express their passion for religion through the niqab. By wearing it, they are heroized by the Salafi men that they idolize, men who incarnate the virility that they seek.

The second group includes women between twenty-two and forty-five years old who differ from women in the previous group in that they have had negative experiences with married life. Often, these women's lifestyles previously diverged from Islamic moral norms, with multiple sexual relations—romantic adventures that end badly. A general profile might include a husband, often of North African origin, who has spent time in prison for offenses such as drug trafficking, a-religious (even if potentially re-Islamized in prison and appearing diligent in prayer). Women in this group include single mothers supporting their children on their own, as the father—or fathers—have long since left their paternal obligations. They also include victims of domestic violence, or even rape, by partners they describe as "psychopaths." Divorces among this group are common and more often initiated by the women.

Women in this second group of niqab wearers sometimes enumerate the wrongs to which they were subjected by their former partners, which they explain by their deviation from Islamic ideals concerning relationships between the sexes. In their present lives, these women strive to follow religious injunctions (with the niqab), in search of happiness and romantic success. In general, these women wish to start their lives over; the niqab might be seen to represent a means of returning to virginity, a fresh start. Salafi men represent the ideal partners in marriage, seen to demonstrate the virtues lacking in previous partners. One common trait, particular to this group, is the stringency of their demands for partners in marriage, which are not only moral but sometimes physical as well. Alexia,* for example, wants her husband to be Moroccan and dark-complexioned and refused an offer of marriage from a white religious convert with light eyes.

Women from this second group, generally, first represent themselves to me as pious and devoted. Such an appearance, however, does not strictly correspond to the complex personalities that render their marriages chaotic and ephemeral (frequently, they are single). The exception in this age group are the women who were re-Islamized along with their husbands, including Kenza Drider,* Sabine, and Sandra. These women stayed married and seem to lead fairly stable romantic lives.

Finally, a third group comprises older women. This group is infrequent in France, although it is widespread in Muslim countries, as I saw during my fieldwork in Southeast Asia and Qatar. I will only sketch it out briefly here. Usually over sixty, these women have lost their feminine appeal after menopause. Veiling their faces lets them minimize their age and continue to exist as potentially desirable women. The niqab, here, plays the role of an aesthetic prosthesis, like a wig or dentures, erasing the effects of time. In Malaysia and Indonesia, this type of niqab wearer is common; such women began to wear the full veil as they approached old age. This use represents another example of the instrumentalization of the full veil to liberate oneself from the gaze of others and to play a new social role.

Reasons for Wearing the Full-Face Veil

Women in my survey give four common reasons for continuing to wear the veil even if it means breaking the law (reasons that involve relationships with men will be addressed in the following chapter).

To Obey and Please God

Women who choose to wear the niqab prioritize their relationships with God, prayer, and intimacy with divinity. The first reason often given to explain the niqab is obedience to God. Wearing the garment represents a show of self-abnegation before Him. Outside of questions of legal conformity, their arguments include expressions such as "to approach Allah" and "to please God." Sandrine Moulères, for instance, describes her feeling of being "closer to God." Alexia,* similarly, defends herself a posteriori against any other motivation:

> I wore the niqab solely because I was convinced that it was my obligation. I wanted to please Allah and to do as much as possible for him.

Covering the body is held to be proportional to faith, as Shamsou explains:

> I wasn't trying to understand. I thought, better to cover more than less. A Hadith, I don't remember which, says "As your faith grows, cover yourself more."

Their actions could be described as a "faith of clothing" that aims to prove piety by outfit, as some of the posts in the Facebook group Niqab Lovers attest: "the niqab is a life of satisfying God" or "if they say that your clothes are too large for fashion, say back: your clothes are too tight for heaven."[9] Heaven is a *postmortem* imaginary projection, a place where the inversion of values must take place. The wearing of the niqab can be understood as a sacrifice undertaken to attain a form of spiritual elevation. In Soraya's words:

> When I wear the full veil, I want to please God. I want to raise myself spiritually.

In this case, self-constraint is intended to appeal to divine election, similar to the corporeal mortifications present in other religions, such as undertaking barefoot pilgrimages or inflicting physical punishments.

The niqab can become a liberating constraint. Sandra, who undertook the *hegira* to the Arab Emirates in 2009 and returned to France in 2020, says:

> In the Emirates, some women wear the niqab because of tradition and some because of belief. The second group also doesn't wear makeup and they also wear gloves. Their gloves are important in understanding their commitment. Women who are converts wear the niqab because of belief; they're sisters.
>
> Today I don't wear the veil anymore and I don't even think of myself as practicing. When I meet a sister in the niqab and gloves she doesn't respond to my salam. Their children don't go out and don't read books with pictures. I came into Islam with a huge faith. I still have my faith but I've separated from the dogma, just like my husband. We came into Islam together and we left it together, me first.

Unlike Carmelite nuns, who also hid their faces beneath a black veil until the Second Vatican Council in the 1960s, niqab wearers do not renounce the world; they only hide their faces and figures. They cut off interactions with the exterior world through a cloth boundary, while still remaining active in society. Another difference from Catholic orders is that these women are isolated from each other. They do not live in monastic communities, but instead individually and independently. It was only after the passage of the 2010 law that some of them came together, virtually, on social media.

For Feelings of Well-Being and Personal Growth

The total cover of the face and skin cannot be reduced simply to religious obedience. It is also linked to physical pleasure and enjoyment. All the women in my study spoke of feelings of well-being and power while wearing the garment. Shamsou, for example, describes first putting on the niqab:

> I feel fully anchored in myself, I feel strong. It's hard to explain, I feel truly confident in myself. I know that men aren't looking at me and lower their heads, women too. It's a sign of respect on its own, and I really feel self-confident. At times like that I know that nothing can stop me—well, except there's always the police!

The full-face veil gives some of its wearers a sense of being valued for themselves. They are seen not as sexualized women, but pious women valued for their interior qualities. They are no longer reduced to what others see. Karima, the daughter of Algerian parents and thirty-one years old when her interview was filmed before the passage of the ban, explains:

> I've been wearing the niqab for sixteen years. For me, when I decided to wear it and to keep it on, I was always doing what I wanted in my life. I

started wearing it very young. I felt good under it. I didn't have any more anxiety about being judged by my physical appearance—that no longer came into play in my relations with others. I liked it and I never wanted to take it off after. I got caught up in it. That's why I've been wearing it so long.

Facial coverings also allow an escape from their physical faults and racial profiling that would stigmatize them for the color of their skin. The visual pressure from the outside world is seen as coercive—it imposes norms—even if niqab wearers are still subject to disapproving looks from people that they encounter in public, the violence of which I witnessed during my time with them.

The notion of freedom from social codes gives rise to an unexpected comparison. In the explanations that they give of their feelings on wearing the full veil, niqab wearers resemble topless sunbathers, although in terms of the way that they display their bodies, the groups appear to be opposite. Both groups of women express a feeling of freedom: the freedom of taking off clothing, on the one hand, and of putting it on, on the other. In a 1995 study, French sociologist Jean-Claude Kaufmann attempted to gauge the pleasure felt by wearers of the monokini.[10] Denying the pleasure that women take from their clothing (or lack of clothing) and actions would mean ignoring the self-expression that these gestures represent. Imagining the niqab as a constraint imposed by men is the counterpart of asserting that women who bare their breasts on a beach are responding to masculine desire. Kaufmann points out that the male companions of topless sunbathers often feel valorized. The same might be said for some niqab wearers' husbands, who benefit from having entirely covered wives and incarnate the pinnacle of Salafi religion—or at least, this is how they are often projected by single niqab wearers. Bare breasts and the niqab both send messages: unconfined and free, or rigorist and pious. Both types of women are seeking fulfillment while still conforming to the criteria of the men that they desire.

Written literature also plays a role in the way that niqab wearers make and perceive their choices. Sold in Muslim bookstores or available for download as .pdfs, manuals exist for the Muslim man and woman to explain how to construct a codified identity and establish models. The editors of such texts have discovered a new publishing niche, alongside more canonical works. Their collections of rules, drawn from the Quran and from Hadiths, establish an ideal that is easy to conform to, presented in the form of the binary between *halal* and *haram*, or licit and illicit. The success of such books can be seen in their translation into French: sample titles include *Ne sois pas triste [Don't be Sad]* and *Soyez la femme la plus heureuse au monde [Be the Happiest Woman in the World]*[11] by the Saudi academic Aidh El Qarni. Muslim editors target a feminine readership, with pink and flowery covers.[12] The women in this study tend to be fond of such works, which touch on all aspects of their daily lives and have become bestsellers in Islamic literature; they are found frequently in their home libraries, as I often observed during interviews.

Juridical recommendations exist as well for men, who must also follow strict guidelines for everyday life. Young Salafi men tend to seek out such rules, as Olivier Roy describes:

> Neo-fundamentalists see in religion a body of dogma, of rites, and of norms defining a code rather than a body of knowledge.[13]

These manuals establish rules starting from questions posed by new and modern religious figures, and Salafi men and women cling to these norms even though they transgress the norms of the rest of the population and even, at least starting with the ban on the niqab, the law.

Books that seek to develop the critical thinking skills of Muslim women are also found in some bookstores: *Faux Hadiths au sujet de la femme [False Hadiths Concerning Women]*,[14] as well as books by the Moroccan scholar Asma Lamrabet on gender equality in the Quran.[15] These books, however, are generally less in favor with niqab wearers, who prefer the reference volume *Recueil de fatwas concernant les femmes [Collection of Fatwas About Women]*, which includes passages that appeal to modern women accustomed to equality between the sexes, such as:

> They [women] are the equals of men, except insofar as the Law differentiates them at the level of the nature of men and women [biological differences]. Beyond that, the ground rule is that they are equal, according to Sheikh Ibn Baz.[16]

An additional work by Aidh El Qarni shows the ideal of the young Saudi woman today as personal, as well as professional, fulfillment: she devotes a portion of her budget to personal development courses with the aim of affirming her self-confidence and working for her own success. All these views are very far from the image of a passive and mistreated woman awaiting her husband's approval for her very existence.

In sum, the religiosity demonstrated by niqab wearers lets them establish themselves in society while nevertheless marking out a difference which, in their eyes, valorizes them, even if they are devalorized in the view of non-Salafi.

For Redemption

If some women act in order to exhibit their religiosity, others are seeking redemption. The full-face veil is also worn for less lofty reasons, to atone for dissolute sexuality or bad conduct. Safiya, a convert to Islam of Cape Verdean origin, born in 1976, describes her journey:

> I was a rebel, a total outlaw, one of those women who didn't want to give in to anything or submit to society or the State. I rejected society completely. But Islam taught me to accept. The niqab fulfills me and makes me happy.

For some of these niqab wearers, the self is positioned as the object of a kind of permanent introspection; egos are interiorized beneath the niqab almost as a form of personal penitence. This quest for redemption is especially evident in the case of the second age group of niqab wearers, those who experienced marital disappointment and who often have children out of wedlock. For some of them, suffering is deeply rooted. Khadija, for example, is a convert to Islam born in 1977; after having worn it for many years, she stopped wearing the niqab after the passage of the law. She explains:

> My mother gave me up and I was put in foster care. I really struggled. I ran away. I made some mistakes, as they say. It was because my family rejected me. I left when I was sixteen I traveled a lot from city to city. I suffered and that's the truth. I went back to the mosques and I prayed. What was it I found in those hard moments? It was the Muslims. I said to myself that I wanted to convert. In Lyon I would say the chahada. I have Allah, I am not alone. But ever since I stopped wearing the niqab I don't feel good. The truth is I want to put it back on.

The niqab can be seen as a form of compensation, helping women seeking dignity find community. It may also be worn in the aftermath of rape, as for Hanane,* born in 1990 to non-practicing Algerian parents and put in foster care at the age of fourteen after suffering abuse and incest at home. She tells of having chosen Islam and the full-face veil as a way out. One of the women in my study most haunted by her past is Naïma S.,* born in 1982 to Algerian parents. She is one of the rare women included here who was married to an abusive man. She recounts seeking to rectify a past that tortures her, a life she considers superficial:

> I was so ignorant, I thought that what mattered to men was physical appearances. I colored my hair and wore makeup. It's a period I regret

very much. It was shaytan *[Satan] who was telling me, you want to get married, ok look, if you do your makeup like this and your hair like that then you'll find a husband. But actually no, not at all. I was so depressed from my sins. The life I have wearing the jilbab and the niqab freed me from my hypocrisy. "When in Rome . . .": I felt like I had to live like the infidels.*

She rebukes herself for various "sins," such as having applied to be a police officer (although she failed the entrance tests). She returns to this failure, which she interprets after the fact, after she has turned to Salafi, as a gift from God and her husband:

I know that Allah put him [my husband] into my path because I was going to die a non-believer. There I was living little life, with the police exams, and God said: no, you'll be complicit in lots of crimes if you succeed. Allah chose another path for me. A few years later I started wearing the jilbab and the niqab, alhamdullilah *[praise God]. There's no better path than to devote yourself to God. I couldn't do that when I was younger and I'm trying to make up for it now.*

To Fight the Objectification of the Body

The niqab represents a reaction against feminine hypersexualization within Western societies: this is another explanation for why some women withdraw so radically from society. The choice to wear the niqab can be framed as a refusal to bend to the aesthetic criteria dictated by media sources such as magazines; the image of the "sexy" woman serves as a counter-model from which some women seek to differentiate themselves. To wear the niqab is to work against the exploitation of the feminine body, a symptom of industrial society. Several such women in my study make use of classic, feminist discourse to justify their life choices, turning the niqab into a source of "empowerment."

Safiya, thirty-four years old, wears a purple niqab and expresses herself in feminist language:

I am a feminist: I defend the rights of women, all women, regardless of nationality, religion, or their ideas about life. I'm protecting all women. I'm against violence against women, I'm against the fact that some women are prostituted. I embrace all feminist causes. For me, a real feminist is a woman who defends women against any man who imposes a certain style of clothing as part of societal norms. That's how you recognize a real feminist! When you call yourself a feminist, that means you disagree with certain of men's principles. That means I'm really, really, really a feminist.

Shamsou, age eighteen, also presents herself as a feminist when speaking of the niqab, which she began wearing a month earlier:

I was always very feminist at heart. I can't stand when a man tells me what to do, especially when there's no real reason. I am very happy to be wearing the niqab. It's my body, it belongs to me, it's all I want to show. Isn't that true freedom, to be able to show what I want to? Because for them freedom's wearing high heels, makeup. No, I'm sorry, they just wear what they want and I wear what I want. Why do I have to make myself dress like them? That's when I'd be oppressed.

Soraya,* in her fifties and of Algerian origin, takes up the old feminist slogan against the objectification of women:

In Islam women are not objects—you know, an object that you just show outside and the whole world can look at all they want. In the Muslim religion, women have value.

Several women explain wearing the niqab as a resistance to the globalization of fashion and beauty norms, and to the physical pressures on Western women. The niqab can represent an exit for women who have been caught up in the world of appearances (the preponderance of beauticians among niqab wearers has already been noted). Hopes for a better life, freed from the constraints of prescribed beauty, are projected onto Islam. Nevertheless, this freedom from feminine norms does not mean that niqab wearers cannot also be "modest fashion victims" in the competition to cover themselves.

The Niqab and the Other

Attraction through Dissimulation

Modesty is a concept fundamental to the new religious movements with which the niqab is associated. Advanced jointly with faith, "modesty"—or the covering of the body's private parts (*awra*)—becomes extended to the entire body. God is everywhere; the body must be hidden from his omniscient gaze. Niqab wearers could be seen to assume the position that they attribute to God: they see without being seen, like God, reinforcing a sense of self-value. Adopting a "dress code" imported from Saudi Arabia is a means of appealing to men with Salafi tendencies, attracted to this spirit of abnegation.

Modesty is held as the highest virtue by which a woman might define herself. But is this a "natural" feeling, or has it been inculcated by Internet theologians? What is the role of individual personalities in the retreat from the world into modesty, in the desire not to be seen or stared at? Is it a drive or an accepted constraint? It is, I argue, both. Muslim women's modesty is constructed in opposition to the supposed permissiveness of Western women, who become counter models to a lifestyle seen as morally superior.

These religious arguments, however, sometimes shade into more self-centered motives. The niqab can serve to exhibit piety with the aim of praise or admiration, and help women gain entry into an elite group to which they seek admission. Hence the reason that more traditional Muslims often condemn public demonstrations of faith: they transgress the humility required of both men and women in Islam. Moreover, this spirit of religious excess explains the preponderance of zealous converts within such practices. The argument for modesty can hide a sentiment of pride.

We have seen that investment in religious clothing can be inversely proportional to real devotional commitment. Some women—although only in a few cases—confided to me that they do not always complete their five daily prayers. Interior faith is more difficult to account for than its social display. This poses the question of sincerity: as the expression goes, "the cowl doesn't make the monk." Is this need for affirmation through visibility sincere, motivated by faith, or only by an existential need to be different? There is, indeed, a paradox inherent here: to display oneself publicly, face hidden, represents a form of exhibiting modesty in order to prove the degree of one's faith. We should not elide that there is a degree of exhibitionism or narcissism at work here. Moreover, a sense of self-value can be stoked by theologians who compare women to precious stones. For example, in Aidh El Qarni's book, *Soyez la femme la plus heureuse au monde*, each chapter takes its title from a gemstone in order to remind readers of the value of pious women, superior to others. Other sheikhs and clerics compare these women to jewels hidden in jewel boxes. In the Tablighi Jamaat, women are lauded during meetings, such as the one I attended in Malaysia, at which an Imam began to speak from behind a curtain: "Many angels are attending today. You are here because Allah has chosen you." Noor, one of the women participating, exclaimed, "We are diamonds! This is why we must be entirely covered, like we're in a precious jewel box so we don't arouse men's greed." The women tend to congratulate themselves.

Sandrine Moulères expresses astonishment at life in Dubai, where she lived for a time. There, women are described as "real pearls":

> There were even mosques in the malls. We could take Quran classes and some beaches were private and set up so that women could swim together without being looked at by strange men. We were treated like real pearls, protected and respected by men who would always let us go ahead waiting in lines, for example.[1]

After having been humiliated in France for wearing the veil, Moulères experienced a sort of narcissistic excitement in Dubai. The place she describes represents an ideal society, one in which men are disciplined and banned from places that are not specifically for them.

An Aesthetic Element

Across several countries in which the full veil is the norm, it quickly becomes evident that the niqab involves certain aesthetic benefits for its wearers. In particular, it minimizes or cancels out differences of age and physical appearance, such as obesity. Old or ugly women do not stand out, and the niqab represents a way of remaining desirable. Lila,* the president of the "Amazons for Freedom" association and a niqab wearer, voices an unexpected argument:

> They [women] are far from being what we imagine. Many of them have nothing remarkable about them; no one would turn to look at them if they weren't veiled. The niqab lets them exist.

The veil comes to suggest an extraordinary beauty, of the kind that would have to be covered in order to avoid illicit relations. The veil operates according to a new logic of attraction—attraction that stems not from physical appearance but from the fantasy to which it gives rise in the male imagination. The disappearance of the female body activates a fantasy of ideal beauty, which often ends in disillusionment at the moment of unveiling.

The niqab also has a fetishistic dimension. It would be highly illustrative to carry out a study on the pleasure it gives its wearers—the sensation of embrace in the texture of its synthetic fabric, for instance. Indeed, niqab wearers often speak of the pleasure of being entirely hidden. The French psychiatrist Gaëtan de Clérambault (1872–1934), who photographed the veils of Moroccan women and elaborated a theory of the eroticization of fabric, described the fetishism of the material that covered women, including their faces. The niqab also resembles the BDSM masks and latex outfits sold in sex shops. We find this same kind of fetishism in the Japanese zentai, a Lycra garment that covers the entire body, leaving nothing exposed. In this full-body outfit, the face, and thus the identity, are entirely hidden, freeing the wearer from social constraints in public spaces.

It is undeniable that the niqab has a seductive side. Yet this is paradoxical, occurring through dissimulation and suggestion. Niqab wearers attract in a way that runs counter to traditional codes of attractiveness. Certain accepted means of feminine attractiveness can also be perceived as signs of subordination. Like the niqab, high heels also work in overdetermined and conflicting ways. By causing imbalance, stilettos tend to make women seem fragile and teetering, potentially vulnerable. It might be argued that they contribute to the objectification of women by causing pain and potentially deforming women's feet. In June of 2019, a movement of Japanese women formed to contest the requirement for high heels at work.

But women who wear high heels generally do not explain it as an imposition. On the contrary, they explain their choice in terms of power and pleasure: they fascinate their interlocutors from their elevated position, their slim and sexualized silhouette, an effect impossible to create with flat-soled shoes. They consider high heels an attractive fashion choice, not a constraint imposed by men. The niqab can work similarly: the woman wearing it captivates her entourage and enjoys her power over others with no external coercion. Would the same harsh critics of the niqab condemn French women in stilettos for their "submission," using the Japanese group as an excuse?

The niqab's public modesty also suggests a private erotic dimension. Samia* shows me her closet, taking out the lingerie and thongs she likes. She prides herself on keeping in touch with her femininity while wearing the niqab, speaking like a connoisseur:

> *I wear lace and silk, thongs, nighties, matching sets, just about everything. Sometimes I buy sets of all different perfumes—I change perfume too often. I want to switch, I never want to stick with just one perfume. It's a fantasy in my life. I know Allah loves beauty. He likes for people to be beautiful.*

Such a demonstrative attitude is rare among French Salafi women (Samia* is Algerian). Most other women speak of their attraction for beauty and attractiveness as part of their pasts, something they ended when they began wearing the full-face veil.

The niqab can also be linked to frustrations of competition between women. During her time wearing the niqab, Alexia* expressed disdain for the women she encountered in the street who wore less clothing than she did. She would have wanted them to be fully covered, not for Islamic moral reasons, but because she saw competition as disloyal:

> *I have a hard time standing women who show off their bodies to attract men. Even if they don't want to see they're automatically attracted. Women inflate men's sex drives. I hate them. I saw one woman who was showing off her big breasts in a tank top. Since I'm flat-chested I hate it even more. I need to possess men. If all women wore the niqab, men would be at our disposal. That's why the niqab isn't just recommended—it's compulsory, even if it's hard to wear.*

A Safeguard Against Desire

Some niqab wearers confess to being tempted by multiple sexual relations. For these women, the niqab provides a barrier against fulfilling their desires outside of marriage. Saliha,* a convert to Islam, twenty-seven years old and of Martiniquan origin, speaks of her attraction to the handsome men she sees in public and of being forced, now, to lower her head because of her religion.

Alexia* enjoys talking about her appetite for men and her irresistible need to attract them, an activity she has given up "thanks" to the niqab which assumes the role of a guardrail for her drives. She told me repeatedly that the niqab lets her escape from her own desires and from her need to be looked at and coveted by men:

> A woman who says she doesn't like to attract men—I don't believe her, she's lying. All women are flattered by male attention. If they say they're not they're hypocrites and liars.

She is sure of herself and assertive when I express doubts about her pronouncements. One day she admits to her own ambition, when younger, of becoming an "escort girl," captivating and possessing men in the absence of any sexual relation. She is, however, shocked to read this confession in one of my articles[2] even though she is protected by the anonymity of the pseudonym "Cindy." She demands that I call her Alexia* in my texts and has fortunately not broken off our contact.

Alexia* attributes this function of regulation to the Islamic religion, which serves as a control for a sex drive she describes as never satisfied: "If I weren't Muslim, there'd be lots of men at home constantly." Saliha* and Alexia* both claim to have succeeded in mastering, through Islam, their obsession with men and their irrepressible desire to attract them.

The Niqab and Matrimony

In Salafi communities, the full veil allows for quick marriages and remarriages. These unions are easier to form and to break when they are not registered with the state. They are finalized before two male witnesses. The bride does not attend the ritual in person; she is represented by a *mahram*. Formalized orally, this Muslim marriage is dissolved by a ritual formula (*talaq*) repeated three times in Arabic by the husband: *anti taliqa, anti taliqa, anti taliqa* (you are divorced), which is then followed by a "widowhood" period of three months to ensure that the woman is not pregnant. In a Salafi context, marriage for pleasure (*zawâj al-mut'a*) is also practiced. The couple tries out life together for a period, with the possibility of separating and starting over afterwards. These unions are ephemeral, lasting only a few months or even a week, and they help explain the number of niqab wearers who have been divorced multiple times or who have children that they raise on their own.

Accelerating Marriages

Unlike their mothers, second- and third-generation daughters are encouraged to go out. They study, succeed, and work. They become independent and insistent on marriage. On the other hand, men in immigrant families are slower socially, leading to major disparities in marriage age even though endogamic union is still given precedence. The social inequalities between men and women lead to a lack of opportunity for marriages. This difficulty can lead to long periods of celibacy. Many practicing women experience sexual abstinence and struggle with solitude. Certainly, there are niqab wearers with long marriages, but these are exceptional. The majority of them have no male partner, or have a succession of short flings, still in search of true love.

Niqab wearers tend to desire and idealize a certain type of man. The niqab stands as a symbol of their piety and their faithfulness, a moral guarantee on the very competitive Muslim marriage market, especially in the Salafi community. Saliha* tells of having regularly been asked for her hand in marriage since she has been wearing the niqab, which never happened to her while she wore the jilbab.

In Search of a Salafi "Prince Charming"

"Prince charming" is a well-known figure in the imagination of the young girl. The French sociologist Jean-Claude Kaufmann's study of single women in search of their "prince charming" shows that the figure is usually accompanied by a traditional representation of the couple and the family;[3] some of his study's participants even actively seek out "dependence on a husband." Perhaps ironically, the total emancipation of Western women has yet to occur, and the traditional division of gender roles is very much still at play.

The Salafi "prince charming" must possess all of the Islamic virtues: he must be a good Muslim, respectful of religious duties, entirely devoted to God and his family, and faithful and responsible. Salafi women seek a pious husband whose gaze is different from other men's. It is not a dominating gaze that reifies them or seeks out other women, but a modest gaze that turns away. The niqab is a sort of test—proof of men's abnegation in favor of God. The problem is that very few men, even among the Salafi, are able to overlook women's physical aspects.

Salafi couples often meet on group social media networks, as well as Muslim dating sites such as muslima.com, where each individual enumerates their moral strengths. These networks allow users to find matches quickly, freeing them from preliminary encounters that would traditionally take place before physically present witnesses. Even marriages are sometimes carried out on Skype or Facebook in the presence of virtual witnesses. Several niqab wearers in my study had virtual ceremonies: like everyone else, the Salafi exist in our post-industrial, consumer society, in which many different types of transactions take place on the Internet with no need to even leave the house. The speed of marriages in the Salafi sphere is impressive. Couples are married without seeing each other in person—after brief virtual exchanges, then telephone conversations. The *mahram* is replaced by a "virtual brother" for women in need of one, such as Alexia* on Facebook, for example.

In May of 2012, Alexia* sends me an email: "Announcing the occasion of my marriage, *alhamdullilah*." Her new husband is a convert to Islam and only twenty-three years old, fourteen years younger than she is. She had spoken to me several days earlier after having met him on a Muslim site. The marriage was effected on the Internet:

> The brothers united on Facebook. I wasn't present, since the woman doesn't need to be there during the niqah [marriage]. A man contacted me through msn in order to arrange the dowry. I asked for Ibn Kathir's Tafsir [Quranic commentary]. All of the brothers came together on Facebook to decree the niqah to the "room."

The new husband, Alexia's* fifth, is introduced as her guide and her mentor in theology:

> Islamically speaking, he's the one who's going to teach me things. I don't really feel the fourteen years' age gap between us. I am blown away by his knowledge of tawhid [God's oneness]. Allah doesn't give that to everyone. I realized I was off-track in my understanding of God's oneness. There are texts that you can't find in bookstores or in mosques but only on the Internet. He sent me tons of .pdfs, he filled me in. No man has ever taken care of me like that. And what he likes in me is the gratitude I show.

The new couple still has not met in person, since the husband lives in the countryside with his mother. Several days later, her excitement has waned:

> Of course I hope I haven't made a mistake by marrying a twenty-three-year-old. I said many salat al-istikhara [prayers for advice] but I'm still naïve. The problem is that in Islam you can't wait too long. Some people can do some preliminary research about their future spouse but how can we, now? We don't know anyone.

Finally, the husband-mentor arrives at her house. He turns out to be a poor partner, however. He spends his days in the living room and lets himself be taken care of. One night he commands her to wax her legs, which causes her to explode:

When my husband asked me to wax I said no even though I'd intended to do so. I don't obey like that, I'm not at his beck and call. He showed no tact at all, he could have asked me nicely. Instead he used religion, he said, I order you. Fine, I'm the one who ordered him to say the talaq *and get out of my house!*

Their cohabitation lasted only two weeks. The extreme quickness of these marriages and their lack of grounding in reality often lead to disappointment. The Muslim website SaphirNews includes a column written by two female psychoanalysts that takes up, among other things, the problems with these Internet unions, addressing the complaints of victims who recount intimate details of their marital lives. The success of this column shows that practicing Muslim women trust psychoanalytic therapy; some of them, including Sandra, Alexia,* and Stéphanie,* are also fans of sophrology and hypnosis.

As another example, Émilie König* pursued her quest for the ideal spouse for a long time. Like others, she used Muslim dating sites. In the spring of 2012, she met the man of her dreams on one of the sites, a Belgian who introduced himself as a "former friend of Bin Laden and the perpetrator of a shooting in London." But he soon disappointed her by sharing a nude photo of her that he had asked her to send on social media (the Salafi also use revenge porn). This setback accelerated her departure for Syria in 2013, where she married a French jihadist with whom she had three children before he was killed in battle.

The Full Veil vs. Masculine Drives

The niqab deprives the male gaze of its pleasure while niqab wearers remain in control of their visual capacities. The gaze is censured for men but allowed for women. The niqab cuts short all undesired male attention as well as men's scopic drive, or scopophilia, the pleasure of possessing the other through the gaze. The Muslim man's lowered gaze is a response to the woman's niqab: a double constraint in the relation between the sexes. These women are not available to male strangers, Muslim or non-Muslim. In the face of this frustration, the latter sometimes become aggressive.

Behind the strong discipline it requires, the niqab also constitutes an authority over men, forbidding them the visual pleasure they could take from women's bodies. Wearing the niqab reverses the direction of domination. Sabine enjoys the sensation:

I have the freedom to choose who can look at me. It's very fulfilling. It's stronger than I am—I can't bring myself to take off the niqab. It's incredible to me that people don't understand that we are happy like this. I'm comfortable in it.

Like the veil, the niqab is described by women who wear it as a tool that mandates respect, keeping men at distance. Véronique,* from Toulouse, explains:

In the street I saw a woman walking wearing a short skirt. I saw how men looked at her. It was awful. I told myself that men were never going to look at me like that.

Some niqab wearers express their disgust at men's freedom to harass women and their disdain for the way men enjoy the female body. Moreover, the majority of them claim to be in favor of the #MeToo movement against sexual harassment. For these women, the niqab provides protection against a society perceived as permissive to street harassment. This is often one of the foremost justifications for wearing the niqab and even the shorter veil. In the words of Shamsou:

It's my body and it belongs to me. You—you, a man—you don't have to come see it. It's to put up barriers because I'm sick of being hit on in public. I feel like I'm in my bubble, I feel protected, nothing can touch me, men lower their gazes.

Some women use the image of meat to describe men's greed for women's bodies and to justify women's desire to escape. Safiya is explicit:

No, I don't want to be displayed, I don't want my body to appear, like some old cut of meat on the shelves.

Shamsou uses the same comparison:

Before, when men looked at me, I felt like a piece of meat that a dog is looking at with its mouth open. But now, well, I'm a piece of meat but I'm very well packaged.

Deeper in these women's stories, the theme of rape arises fairly frequently, often spontaneously evoked after a few sessions: generally repeated rape, often in childhood by a family member. The niqab might also be seen as a manner of putting oneself back together. The full veil permits women, not only to keep their distance from the male gender, but also to choose which men have access to their bodies. Hanane* and Naïma* both survived incest and rape which were subsequently denied by their mothers. In such cases, the niqab can be a reaction to the impunity of the rapists. Hanane* received no justice: her case against her stepfather was dismissed. In Naïma's* case, her mother committed her to a psychiatric hospital when she began to report being raped by her father.

A Constraint on Husbands

The niqab also represents a form of spousal control, imposing proper Islamic behavior on husbands. Most often, it is the women who force their husbands (if they are married) to accept the niqab. The men are often resistant or consent grudgingly; for them, the niqab represents a form of moral coercion over them, except in the case of affirmed Salafi men for whom a woman wearing the niqab serves to protect their image of their own piety.

Certain niqab wearers are zealous propagandists for Islamic morality and seek to control their husband's sexuality. Samia,* thirty-six years old and of Algerian origin, speaks of the pressure to which her niqab allows her to submit her husband:

I don't like for my husband to look at other women. My husband used to be "super cool," as the French say. He'd been living in that society since age twenty and he's adjusted to being here—parties, going out, girls. But I made a sacrifice for him and I want him to make the effort for me, to prove his love. We had neighbors, Christians, and he would kiss them on the cheeks, like the French do. I explained to him, it's not that I'm jealous but that's not allowed in my religion.

Of course, this power over men is not simple or universal. The women who exercise authority over their husbands are not in the majority, as we saw in the second group of niqab wearers outlined earlier, those scarred by their bad experiences of married life. The niqab also serves them as a source of reparation after having been badly treated by their male partner(s). These women are still in search of the ideal man, someone in keeping with traditional stereotypes of strength and protection. In a sense, the niqab might play the role of a substitute for the ideal spouse, protecting and completely enveloping. The niqab would replace the absent man, the husband impossible to find. But men do not always understand the signal that the niqab sends. They believe it means the woman is untouchable and might think that she is already married or is self-sufficient, using the niqab as a deterrent. They cannot imagine a place for themselves in the relationship that pre-exists them, between the woman and her niqab. This symbiosis might explain some women's difficulties in finding a long-term partner. The day she took off the niqab after five years of wearing it, Alexia* declared frankly: "I'm giving up. It's not going to help me find a guy."

The Niqab's Opponents

The full-face veil is both fantasized and instrumentalized by Islam's detractors. It has always been a source of inspiration for numerous editorialists, thinkers, and essayists who have very little knowledge of the empirical facts but who are convinced that it represents a manifestation of a proselytizing and dominating form of Islam. Exclusion and demonization of Muslims has been common in France since the Algerian War. Islam has further become a source of anxiety after the 1979 Iranian Revolution, also aggravated by the Iran-Iraq War (1980–1988), the September 11 attacks, the formation of the Islamic State in Syria and Iraq in 2014, and the Paris terrorist attacks in January and November of 2015.

Books containing the stories of female victims of Islam often sport cover illustrations of niqabs or the Afghan *chadri*, even when these garments do not appear in the stories they tell. These narratives often flirt with fiction but present themselves as fact, even though few bear the real name of the author. They are often co-written with journalists with an eye toward sales figures. The first in a series of them, *Jamais sans ma fille* [*Not Without my Daughter*], by Betty Mahmoody, was published in French in 1988.[4] The cover photo depicts the gaze of a woman surrounded by a black niqab. And yet, in the book, the narrator never wears the garment, which indeed was no longer the custom in the Islamic Republic of Iran at the time. Another example is Zeina's testimony in *Sous mon niqab*,[5] co-written with the journalist Djénane Kareh Tager,[6] which corresponds to stereotypes about niqab wearers. This book caters exactly to what French society imagines Muslim women to be, with their "submission" to their husbands. All the clichés are present: the jealous husband, forcing his pregnant wife to wear the niqab, with violent slaps. The vocabulary is chosen to disgust the reader. The book was published in May of 2010, six months before the ban on facial coverings was passed, and after public controversy in the country had been swirling for a year. Given the impossibility of checking any sources (the protagonist, Zeina, cannot be found), it is not difficult to imagine a fictional account, constructed to prime public opinion for the passage of the ban. Such narratives have little to do with actual niqab wearers, and we cannot gauge the verisimilitude of these supermarket bestsellers. Anti-niqab clichés have become products of contemporary consumption.

Violence Against Niqab Wearers and Their Children

Aggression against Muslim women has skyrocketed after the passage of the ban in 2010. Around this time, Islamophobic speech infiltrated public spaces, normalizing insults and physical aggressions by ordinary citizens, with more checks carried out and more fines leveled by police officers. Every woman in my study noted a rise in aggression toward them under the pretext of the law. They recount sexist and degrading insults, being spit on and threatened, and attempts to forcibly remove their veils. As Latifa, from the suburb of Grigny, south of Paris, attests:

> *The law did nothing besides increase racism, which is more overt now. People don't hide it when they insult us, and the insults truly are racist.*

Without recourse to the police, most women gave up filing complaints. Those who did go to the authorities saw their complaints turned against them and were themselves sentenced instead, as Sophie* was. Several instances of violence committed by ordinary citizens, both Muslims and non-Muslims, a few months before the ban was passed, demonstrate that such incidents increased due to the rise of controversy in June 2009:

> KARIMA: *I would take public transportation in the morning. A woman jumped on me and attacked me. Two people held her back. She was amazingly, extremely violent. What's funny is that she was shouting all the things the politicians were saying at the time: "It's not in the Quran, this is for women's freedom, women's dignity." All she was thinking was that if she got it off me, I'd be happy. I was defending myself, all I wanted was for her not to tear off my niqab.*
>
> KHADIJA: *Recently at Croix de Chavaux [a metro stop in the Paris suburb of Montreuil], a woman, a Tunisian woman, told me: "You offend us." I said, "Excuse me, madame, are you talking to me?" "Yes you, Fantômas."[7] Every time you go out, someone insults you: "Fantômas, you're ugly." Once I left the house to get the 122 [bus]. Three Frenchmen spat in my face. I turned right around.*
>
> LOUISA: *I've been spat on, assaulted, I've got tons of friends who've gotten beaten up. I even knew a girl who was attacked with a knife.*

The niqab wearers in my study report being harassed and assaulted by women. According to their accounts, the most representative among their attackers are women over the age of fifty, often overweight and disheveled, who use coarse and sexist language.

Niqab wearers recount the bullying and violence to which they are subject at length. Saliha* even outfitted herself at Decathlon [a sports store] and a gun shop to protect herself:

> *I'm afraid of being assaulted. I carry tear gas in my bag and I have an alarm. If they're going to assault me I'd have to defend myself. I bought*

boxing gloves and a punching bag. I'm fighting for my freedom and for self-defense. Before I never imagined I'd have to learn self-defense but after the law was passed, I have to. Now I practice boxing, I work out at home, I lift weights. It's just incredible that in my own country I feel in such constant danger.

Mothers wearing the niqab report having been assaulted by angry passersby or fined by police in the presence of their children. These children witness the verbal and physical violence, as well as the humiliations, that their mothers suffer. Stéphanie,* from Toulouse, recounts:

The last time, they called me a whore. That's unacceptable, especially in front of my daughter. When I was arrested by the police, I cried in front of her and she kept saying, "Stop crying, mom." It's heartbreaking.

The police also conduct humiliating pat-downs and body searches, feeling women's private parts in public or intimidating them in the presence of their children. Sabine, one of the women who has been wearing the niqab for the longest period, was deeply shaken by a police interrogation to which she was subjected in the presence of her daughters, in 2014, in the eastern Paris suburb of Montreuil:

I was at the bus stop during Ramadan. The police came to check my papers. I had forgotten my ID and they wanted to take me to the station. I was pregnant and had my two daughters with me. They began folding up the stroller and taking my bag. I broke down and started crying. My oldest daughter had a tantrum and started screaming. They said my husband was forcing me. Then they dropped it and fined me. I got the ticket six months later: 172 euros.

Lila,* from the "Amazons for Freedom" organization, tells a similar story from February 2012:

A French convert from Troyes, who wants to go by the name Oum Asrar, was arrested by the police. In the van she was separated from her child, a one-month-old baby. He wasn't wearing his seatbelt. Why? For a minor infraction and after she agreed to state her identity. She was traumatized— she'd been raped as an adolescent. She felt like she was reliving the same thing.

Children taken with their mothers to the police station have the potential to react defensively, rejecting the police. Naïma S.,* arrested with her three-year-old son on September 28, 2016, in the suburb of Aubervilliers, describes:

> *They put me in the cell with my son. He said, "Now we're in* habs *[in jail, Arabic slang]." He was shocked, he kept saying, "we're in* habs, *we're in* habs." *I said yes, we're in* habs *because mom is wearing the niqab. What shocked me was that they took my purse, they took my personal possessions, they even took his little plastic lion! A few weeks later he said to me, "The cops are mean, they put us in* habs."

These traumatic memories will later leave a resentment toward the police and the state, for the son as well as the mother:

> *The police, I'm not going to lie, they've always hated us. They hate immigrants and they hate Islam and they hate Muslims. It's been going for a long time. They've always hated us, even before the Islamic State existed. The more we try to follow Islam, the more it bothers them, the more trouble they give you.*

These women can no longer enter public schools to collect their children. In a shift toward autarchy, many have decided to take them out of school and to undertake their education themselves. Like their mothers, the children find themselves deprived of socialization, with limited access to the exterior world. In the majority of cases, the women are divorced and raising children alone, and they did not wear the niqab before the law was passed.

A Reaction to the Ban

In France today, niqab wearers are increasingly rare in public. Although this might indicate that the law has been a success, the reality is—as always—more complicated.

A Boomerang Effect

The October 11, 2010 law has had a persuasive effect rather than a dissuasive one. The reaction it has provoked is the opposite of what was intended. Not only do the majority of niqab wearers not obey the ban, but the law has reinforced their desire to cover themselves completely. The ban has had the effect of catalyzing visible expressions of the Muslim religion. After October 2010, more women veiled their faces, wanting to distinguish themselves as rigorists. The niqab ban has led to its own transgression, attracting new women to the Salafi community. The full-face veil has shifted from a sign of piety to a signal of assertiveness. The niqab is even more desirable for young women in search of an anti-conformist identity. It has become a sign of protest against Western societies in which permissiveness, when it comes to clothing, is a social asset.

The ban has also led to a rise in the number of adolescent converts to Islam. In search of self-affirmation, these new converts wear the jilbab, and sometimes the niqab, immediately after converting. Many niqab wearers in France are converts—I estimate around half, a surprising portion, considering that converts represent only 2% of French Muslims. As it becomes demonized, the niqab becomes all the more attractive: it is a voluntary step, part of the process of overcoming obstacles. The ban also fed into the logic of victimization, pushing Muslims to rise up against injustice.

The ban on religious symbols in schools in 2004 led to a similar boomerang effect. When schoolgirls had to remove their headscarves in the classroom, more of them tended to wear it outside: the law gave rise to emulation. Some Muslim middle- and high-school students embraced this exclusion, continuing their studies through correspondence courses or in private Catholic schools considered more tolerant. This period also saw the rise of Muslim schools. Young Muslim women began to wear the hijab in everyday life, outside of school, even when they had not worn it before. Headscarves had previously been worn, primarily by first-generation female migrants from former French colonies who came to France in the 1970s to join their husbands, but headscarves for young Muslim women grew increasingly common in public spaces.

Because I started my research in the fall of 2008, I was able to watch as enthusiasm for the niqab rose, beginning with the 2009 controversy, and increased with media attention. For the most part, these women started wearing the garment after the passage of the ban or during the period of highly mediated controversy that preceded it. The first niqab wearers, who wore it before the law was passed, in general, behaved very differently from the more self-assured, newer wearers, often choosing to limit excursions out of the house or to do so only discreetly. Since its ban, wearing the niqab has become a gesture of protest in public spaces and a sign of willed disobedience.

Niqab wearers themselves confirm the existence of a causal relationship, making a conscious link between the ban and their decision to start wearing the niqab. Ourida, wearing a heavy black niqab, was filmed at the twenty-ninth annual meeting of French Muslims in Le Bourget in 2012:

> *Humans have always desired the forbidden. They banned the niqab and many sisters, even converts, learned about the value of the niqab and of Islam. There have been many conversions since last year, praise God.*

Or as Shamsou, who donned the niqab after the law's passage, says:

> *If there hadn't been the law, I don't think I would have thought of wearing it—I'd have said: it's allowed so it's not so important. But if it's banned, maybe that's for a reason. We have to wear it. We can't ever know—perhaps Allah is testing us. Anyway, that's why I wear it. I'm not planning on taking it off any time soon, inshallah.*

Even before the ban, the controversy that arose in June of 2009 had motivated other women, such as Asma, age nineteen, born to Algerian parents, to wear the niqab. In our 2010 interview, she explained:

> *A year ago I wouldn't have imagined myself wearing the niqab. I didn't even know what it was or why they wore it. Little by little there was the controversy and I got interested, I talked to women who were wearing it. I went to go see, I read books. I saw that they had their reasons, they were happy and sane, they weren't crazy, they weren't submissive.*

Alexia* recounts her decision having also been influenced by politics, in particular by André Gerin, the politician who headed the parliamentary study commission to look into the full veil in June 2009:

> *Paradoxically, it wasn't a religious man who led me to the conviction [to wear the niqab]. It was a man who could be called Islamophobic, cruel, everything else. That was the beginning of what got me here.*

Even a woman like Naïma S.,* whose life is more difficult, makes the connection between the controversy and her determination to wear the full veil:

> *When I started wearing the veil, and then the sitar too, it was during the Sarkozy years. It was the middle of the controversy around the ban on the niqab. It didn't make me back off.*

Saliha* taunts an imaginary public on camera, even addressing the French president (at the time):

> *The more you attack us, the more Islamophobic laws and restrictions on Muslims, the stronger it's going to get, the more we'll go back to real Islam [. . .] Before the law, I was what I think the majority of Muslims are like. They try to have it both ways. I mean, they follow French law while still being Muslim. For me that's one foot in hell, one foot in heaven. When you try to reconcile the two, at some time or another you sin without even meaning to. It's dangerous. That's why it's better to go back to true Islam because France doesn't accept us. [. . .] I want to thank Monsieur Sarkozy, thank you so much, for having made me really think hard about the full-face veil. And I'm not the only one. Some sisters took it off. But others, like me, decided to wear it. Thanks, Sarkozy!*

Abou Mohamed, who owns one of the "Islamic" stores on the Rue Jean-Pierre Timbaud in Paris's 11th arrondissement, also credits Sarkozy with an increase in business and profits, starting in December of 2010. In 2020, bookstores along this street confirm that they continue to sell the niqab at a rate of around a dozen garments per month.

The Rise of the Jilbab

If, today, the niqab has almost disappeared after its rise, the jilbab, on the other hand, has spread. The jilbab covers the entire body, and the niqab is the article of clothing tied around the forehead; the niqab, in other words, is an accessory to the jilbab. Worn alone (without a niqab), the jilbab lets the face be seen but gives the woman the same silhouette as a niqab wearer. We should note that women who wear the jilbab do not behave the same way as some of the niqab wearers. They are often not as disinhibited and do not wear makeup, unlike some women who wear the niqab and use kohl and mascara. They are often more advanced in religious study and practice. This outfit spread widely after the ban of face coverings in French territories, although it had been rare even before the 2010 law. It has even become fashionable in France among young women who seek to display their rigorism and their adherence to the literalist Salafi movement. Another outfit variation consists of pulling the jilbab up to the chin and down to the eyebrows to reveal fewer than ten centimeters of the face (between the mouth and the eyes). Some women also wear large black sunglasses, creating a kind of makeshift niqab in order to avoid fines. After the beginning of the COVID-19 pandemic, in spring of 2020, the surgical mask recommended (or even required) by health authorities was in some cases jubilantly adopted (whereas before it was not, having no Muslim meaning). Covering the face became a civic-minded gesture.

Resistance

In the eyes of niqab wearers, the verbal and physical attacks that they suffer in public spaces justify the soundness of their clothing choices. The police searches, and assaults from ordinary passersby, as well as a sense of general hostility, strengthen their determination. Only a small portion of less perseverant, new niqab wearers have stopped wearing the veil. But the majority of them assert, at least initially, not wanting to take it off. Here, for example, are several statements from single women in 2011 and 2012:

> LAURENCE: *I decided to keep wearing my niqab and going out in it despite the risk, and to fight with the other sisters who wear it to repeal the law depriving us of our freedom.*
> HANANE*: *I'm comfortable wearing it. I tried to go out without it but I just couldn't.*
> KARIMA: *I'm so attached to it that I can't imagine not wearing it.*
> HIND AHMAS*: *It never crossed my mind to take off my niqab.* Inshallah *I'll die wearing it.*

And yet Hind Ahmas* would stop wearing the niqab several years later. In 2016, after her decision to do so, she explains her fatigue bitterly:

I'm not trying to convince anyone anymore. It's energy spent for nothing because people like that are never going to accept us. What they call women's freedom is just vulgarity, reality TV shows that make me want to throw up. And then to say that I—that I don't have the right to dress how I want!

In the face of the ban, niqab wearers argue that they obey a higher, divine law. They perceive themselves as superior to other citizens and reject human laws. There is a logic of elitism at work here: some women refer to the majority of mortals using deprecatory terms such as "creatures of this worldly life"[1] or "docile sheep."[2] The hostile reactions that this position provokes only serve to further demonstrate the necessity of breaking with society. Niqab wearers are reaffirmed in their choices to wear the niqab despite the ban and to love God when this is forbidden; their piety becomes heroic and is expressed in a spirit of resistance. As Saliha* asserts in 2012:

It's a religious requirement, obviously. But now the niqab for me is also a form of resistance. A resistance against the illegal law depriving me of my freedom.

Alexia* speaks similarly in 2016 after five years of wearing the full veil:

The law had a negative effect in two ways. It had a negative effect on women because they felt oppressed, shut in, rejected, and they suffered. And because it led other women to wear the veil as a form of revolt.

The Islamic scholar Mohammed Hocine Benkheira also takes up debates around the niqab's moral reward:

The attitude of women who wear the niqab and who contest the law of a state that forbids the niqab is understandable. This attitude of contention could be considered meritorious.[3]

Yannick Danio, the national representative for the police union SGP-FO, explains the wearing of the niqab after it was banned:

It's a form of resistance no matter what. In relation to a law or in relation to a text, it's logical that people who are against it would come together to show their discontent and to join the resistance against the text.[4]

Yet not all police officers share Danio's judgment. Police checks and searches of women wearing the full veil in majority Muslim neighborhoods tend to escalate and lead to violence. Police treatment of Cassandra Belin, age twenty, unleashed riots in the suburb of Trappes (west of Paris), on July 18, 2013, which were followed by the storming and seizure of the police station by the town's inhabitants. In Toulouse, urban violence inflamed the working-class neighborhood of Bellefontaine au Mirail from the fifteenth to the eighteenth of April 2018, following the arrest of a niqab wearer who was pinned to the ground by two police officers. Danio had already spoken in 2011 of the difficulty surrounding the issuing of fines for facial coverings, predicting future unrest:

> *It's easy to imagine that in certain "hot" neighborhoods, sensitive neighborhoods, a woman covering her face gets stopped by police, it's easy to imagine how it could end. There'll be a mob. After, outrage, rebellion. Then there'd be reinforcements, with all the violence that could generate on both sides. That's really not something we need.*[5]

The Niqab as Jihad

Over a short span of time, wearing the niqab has become such a daily trial (*mihna*) that a comparison with jihad seems necessary. Resisting French law is a fight to please God, as jihad in Islam prescribes. It is first, a major jihad (abnegation, work on the self) that is transformed for a few into minor jihad, or armed jihad, the object of worldwide media attention. Saliha* frames a comparison between the negative reactions she provokes and jihad:

> *Now when I go out, it's like I'm embarking on a jihad. I know that I'm going to be insulted, I know that there'll be looks.*

Alexia* expresses much the same thing:

> *The act of going out in public with the niqab and the sitar, having the sword of Damocles over your head at all times, it's jihad. It's jihad because we're resisting in order not to take it off, despite the pressure on us. But in France it's not armed jihad. When people talk about jihad, they immediately see something frightening. But it's just self-defense. Anyone would defend themselves if they were attacked.*

For Salafi Muslims, niqab wearers are elevated to the rank of martyrs who have sacrificed their own comfort and who confront a society hostile to their form of devotional abnegation. Any discrimination they face only further elevates them for this group.

Organizations Against the Law

Attracting some women to Salafi was not the ban's only effect. It also led to the creation of three small groups that formed out of social media connections: "Citizens for Freedom," founded by Rachid Nekkaz; "Amazons for Freedom," by Lila;* and Forsane Alizza, by Mohammed Achamlane. Each of these organizations was founded to fight the law and offered women a way to contest it. But they also sought control of niqab wearers who were originally independent and isolated from each other, and rivalries sprang up.

The Franco-Algerian businessman Rachid Nekkaz founded the organization "Touche pas à ma constitution" ("Don't touch my constitution") in 2010, and then "Citizens for Freedom," with Kenza Drider* heading it. The group offered to pay the fines of women sentenced under the ban. The media attention it helped attract would encourage some women to break the law, as Hind Ahmas,* a member of the group, explains:

> Women can take different attitudes towards the police: there are those who don't want to leave their houses, and those who go out and don't care because they know that if they get fined they can send it to Rachid Nekkaz to pay. I'm in the second group. When I learned that he'd pay the fines, I decided to go out in the niqab. I have rights and I'm going to exercise them.

With Nekkaz's aid, the niqab wearers in this organization mobilize republican and democratic principles in the legal sphere to oppose what they consider an injustice. These women argue against the state's role of domination, and they are determined to appeal their cases in court and reclaim their rights. Because it occurs in the legal sphere, this process could be considered as running counter to Salafi ideology.

On September 22, 2011, Nekkaz organized a press event in front of the town hall in the town of Meaux, on the occasion of the kickoff of Kenza Drider's* candidacy for president. Drider took the stage before a crowd of journalists, referring to the constitution in order to justify repealing the law and promising to fight the state on democratic grounds. Seven years later, in his book *Le Voltaire du niqab*,[6] published in Algeria in 2018, Nekkaz tells of his satisfaction in being able to pay the fines of women stopped in public. The payment of fines for which Rachid Nekkaz takes credit does not correspond to reality as I saw it. The majority of fined niqab wearers claim not to have benefited from any aid from Nekkaz. They recount having received no response to messages sent to the organization's office. Only a few highly publicized cases received assistance.

"Amazons for Freedom" was created by Lila* and boasted three hundred members and thousands of supporters by February 2012. It was in competition with Nekkaz's group from the beginning. Lila* also decided to fight on legal grounds. Her legal training allowed her to give confident advice to fined women over the phone.

Another militant group fighting the law, Forsane Alizza, was founded by the charismatic Mohamed Achamlane and is discussed earlier.

The Niqab as Deviance

The American sociologist Howard Becker's theory of deviance can help frame the phenomenon of the full veil as a deviant behavior, starting from the moment of its ban. As Becker reminds us, deviance comes about through society:

> Social groups create deviance by instituting norms whose infraction constitutes deviance and by applying these rules to particular people and labeling them as outsiders.[7]

Starting with the 2010 law, any woman wearing the niqab might be considered deviant. Niqab wearers labeled as deviant are threatened by some citizens who take on the responsibility of putting them back in line, according to a basic binary: they are the offending parties because they are breaking the law. In Becker's argument, all societies set norms that have moral connotations. Certain actions are encouraged (the "good") and others are forbidden (the "bad").

In the cases of some women who began wearing the niqab after the ban, deviance itself can be even more attractive than a sense of religious belonging. In the order of transgressors that Becker establishes, niqab wearers fall into the same group as homosexuals and drug addicts: those who "develop full-blown ideologies explaining why they are right and why those who disapprove of and punish them are wrong."[8] Women who wear the niqab do not see themselves as deviant. Instead, they experience police mistreatment and insults as injustices and think their adversaries are wrong. They feel misunderstood. None of them, including the women who have stopped wearing the niqab, recognize the legitimacy of the ban.

These women become "outsiders," foreigners in the dominant society into which they were born. This is the feeling described by Alexia,* looking back on her past wearing of the niqab:

> *I wore the niqab for almost five years. I was into the extreme, into both their clothing style and the way of thinking and rejecting others. In that*

milieu, you don't think you're extremist. You just think you're right, and that's what makes all the difference.

The law creates deviance and accelerates the identification of these women as outsiders who oppose the majority upholding the norm. Niqab wearers tend to flaunt the reason for their deviance and display their disobedience of the rules. As Safiya exclaims:

We live our lives in total freedom. We're maybe even more free than it would seem since we don't bend to the rules of society!

At the time of the ban, very few women swapped their niqab for a surgical mask, since the latter had no significance in Islam and was not a sign of deviance. Masks were worn only when absolutely necessary—to enter a bank, for instance. As Becker points out, it is important to take into account who designates what is deviant—the society as a whole that seeks to uphold the laws and is responsible for reminding "outsiders" of their deviance: "Whether an act is deviant, then, depends on how other people react to it,"[9] Becker writes. The niqab is a good example of this principle. A norm in certain Gulf countries, it becomes deviant in Europe—due to the ban, a symbol of deviance itself. Niqab wearers became lawbreakers due simply to their view of norms. The law's supporters, in Becker's words, became the keepers of the moral order; attacks on women who are veiled are linked to morals and propriety. The French feminist writer Élisabeth Badinter is a staunch opponent of the veil. She has invoked moral arguments against the full veil[10] since the beginning of the controversy, calling for a boycott of brands that sell the hijab and "launch themselves into Islamic fashion."[11]

At the opposite end of the spectrum, the French sociologist Michel Wieviorka cautions against the degradation of French laicity. He notes that laicity, when it comes to Islam, should not mean making it into a foreign religion but, on the contrary, allowing its integration and the freedom of religion mandated by the 1905 law separating church and state:

Any other political response, even beyond moral judgment, can only radicalize Muslim citizens, or in any case marginalize them, sometimes pushing them into extremity and locking them into closed communities, excluding or demonizing them.[12]

A Salafi Subculture

Some of the niqab wearers profiled here share mainstream characteristics: as modern women, they live their sexuality freely. They have experienced nightclubs, alcohol, flirtation, and men. Then they embrace Salafi, which like all subcultures has its codes, its language, its means of recognition, and its dress code. The path recommended by these movements is similar to ideologies of personal development in that it advocates self-control and self-fulfillment. French sociologist Raphaël Liogier points out this group's hypermodern tendencies[13] and even compares it to New Age movements.

We find a taste for provocation among girls from more affluent families. In 2005, the year following the school ban, Olivier Roy examined the question of the veil in the context of individualist self-assertion:

> Adolescents' intentions to assert themselves by wearing provocative clothing is a banality in secondary schools, but the affair of the veil has been experienced as the penetration of the school system by Islam. A girl wearing the veil wants simultaneously to assert herself as an individual, escape from the social constraint of her milieu by adopting a sign that grants her both value and autonomy, make herself noticed, affirm a form of authenticity, and on and on.[14]

Like the jazz musicians Becker studies, who assume anti-conformist behaviors to set themselves apart, the Salafi also wish to set themselves apart from others by their way of being. This is how we might interpret the acts carried out by Forsane Alizza, such as the spectacle of Mohamed Achamlane burning the penal code in a public square. This act represented a feat that would come to be memorable, much like guitarists who burn their instruments—Jimi Hendrix burning his guitar on stage in Monterey, California, in 1967. Fire is used to captivate the public. The Quran, too, has been burned in the same type of spectacular ritual by the American pastor Terry Jones in 2011.

The Salafi might be considered the new anti-conformists of French society. They cannot be reduced to their religion alone. To shock and to contradict the bourgeois is not only the domain of the anarchist London punks of the 1970s, but, today, also of those who adhere to a visible religion, such as Islam, which has come to occupy the position of "the shocking." Some niqab wearers turn to Islam because it represents a deviant identity. In Roy's words:

> Religion seems odd to the secularist if it is not confined to the private sphere. And this "oddity" has a power of attraction over some young people who are seeking to break off from society rather than to integrate it [. . .] They latch on to symbols that scare people (the burqa, turban, and of course weapons, with a predilection for cutlasses and knives) [. . .] They seek out radicalism for its own sake.[15]

Niqabs, Piercings, Tattoos

If piercings and tattoos are a form of marking ownership of one's own body for many young people, a form of emancipation from parents, the same might be said of the full veil and the embrace of Salafi ideology. Many of the women in my study had tongue or nose piercings, such as Kenza Drider,* who wears a gold, bird-shaped piercing in her nostril. The nose piercing is widespread among Salafi women, even if some of them have stopped wearing it. Shamsou recounts having worn ear gauges and pierced her nostril and tongue. Laughing, she expresses her juvenile opposition to maternal authority, a common thread among young Salafi:

> *My mother isn't a fan of it. She doesn't want me to wear the veil and she doesn't want me to dye my hair. I mean, it's a little bizarre. My style hasn't changed. I'm still into dyeing my hair, I like to express myself, to wear makeup. It's for at home, for me. No one sees but me.*

These young women have succeeded in using Islamic symbols to set themselves apart, as they would have done in becoming punks, goths, or even Satanists (all these movements dress, generally, in black).

Simple skin markings, like piercings and tattoos, have lost their subversive dimension and become commonplace. Salafi identity, conferred through the aesthetic of the black niqab, constitutes an effective anti-conformism and opposition to society. The niqab is often a means of assertion for adolescents who resist established order. Marking themselves as rebels, they enjoy recounting their daring confrontations with the police.

Seen another way, the turn to Salafi could be understood as an initiation rite, with the niqab as physical proof of transgressing norms and enjoying the forbidden. Never, in any case, does it have to do with "submission."

Finally, this feeling of power through facial veiling takes other forms as well—black bloc activists, for example, who attract attention during protests with their signature t-shirts and black balaclavas.[16] Niqab wearers adopt a similar aesthetic: the niqab and jilbab, most often black, might be compared to the balaclava and to other anarchist clothing. Both groups are simultaneously invisible (they hide their identities) and visible or even extra visible (as adherents to an ideology). Both groups display their identities visibly in order to send a message: they project a different model of society, one that is both utopian and set against current versions of authority. Both styles of clothing and disguise appeal to a similar aesthetic and visual culture.

The Niqab and Disappearance

In his work on self-disappearance, French sociologist David Le Breton studies the manner in which some young people withdraw in order to escape the constraints of identity and protect themselves from the outside world. These manifestations of disappearance can be relatively harmless, such as sleep or video games in which the players lose themselves. Others are more dramatic, such as running away, risk-seeking behavior, suffocation games, or violence intended to induce a coma. Le Breton's description of escapist behavior is especially interesting:

> Consequently, the individual refuses all social recognition, existing among others as a ghost, a shadow detached from its person [. . .] they slide from person to persona—in other words, in Latin etymology, to a mask—without anyone behind it to incarnate and give it a face. There's nothing left behind, there's no one there.[17]

The notion of no longer being anyone suits some women who wear the niqab. Like those who voluntarily disappear, they are looking for a way to abandon their identity and escape society through the black veil that hides their facial expressions. Émilie König* and Véronique* define the niqab as a second skin beneath which they are erased, and ultimately both of them did choose to disappear, the first in Syria and the second in Birmingham.

Several times during my interviews with niqab wearers, I was reminded of anorexia in the way that they expressed their erasure and their will to be invisible in society (even while showing off their disappearance). Both cases, the niqab and extreme thinness, manifest a desire to master the body and submit it to a kind of "tyranny." Both groups inflict privations through self-control: food for anorexics, sun and social relations for niqab wearers. The women who opt for such bodily discipline call themselves free, feminine, and feminists, even though they constrain themselves. The obsession with thinness to which many niqab wearers, like other women, have succumbed (let us remember the high percentage of beauticians among them) leads them to attempt control over their own bodies. Le Breton compares anorexia in young girls to an ascetic practice, a description that might also apply to the niqab wearer and her niqab:

> Ascetic practices reinforce the feeling of identity in convincing them that they possess exceptional resistance and will [. . .] They feel exceptional. Anorexia gives them a prosthetic identity that is all the more important because it is contested by their parents and doctors. A negative

identity thus gives them individuality and the feeling of existing that is due as much to their interior combat against hunger as it is to the trouble caused inside the family circle [. . .] Among the multitude of possible meanings, anorexia also takes on that of the disappearance of the self into nothingness, in the quest for infinite thinness associated with purity, a will to escape a body become translucent, to escape all social links by becoming invisible.[18]

Both anorexia and wearing the niqab are associated with the refusal of the body. Like the anorexic, a woman wearing the niqab is a challenge to the hypersexualization of women in Western society and the pleasure of the male gaze. The idea of becoming asexual and disappearing from society appeals to both groups of women. Anorexia and wearing the niqab represent two ways of escaping female beauty norms. Anorexia can be linked to traumatic events such as childhood sexual abuse, which is also the case for many women who choose to veil their faces. Like anorexia, the niqab functions as a cleansing.

Radicalization

Long underestimated, the number of women among the ranks of jihadists is today well documented. But few thinkers make the connection between the oppressive measures that target veiled women and their commitment to fighting elsewhere. I was able to witness the deterioration of social relations among some niqab wearers who ultimately became radicalized. Radicalized Salafi designate "the other" using the derogatory term infidel and refusing to share in their values. They demonstrate a will to display their anti-conformism, to rise above the crowd and feel superior as a way of bolstering self-esteem.

The Law as Pretext for *Hegira*

Police and civilian harassment have led some niqab wearers—initially just perceived as different—into processes of self-exclusion. Some of them have been fully radicalized and even carried out violent radical acts. The harassment that they suffer only strengthens their desire for autarchy, which is also reaffirmed by Salafi ideology. I witnessed retrenchments of this sort that led some women to leave France for Syria. The law pushed such women into finding places where they felt that their ideologies were more welcome and to undertake *hegira*. Some of them liken the hostility to Islam and the niqab in France to what Muhammad faced when he was persecuted at Mecca and forced into exile in Medina in the year 622, a historic moment ("hegira") in the foundations of Islam that marks year 1 of the Muslim calendar. For Muslims, *hegira* is a command.

As the Tunisian psychoanalyst Nédra Ben Smaïl explains:

> In Europe, some Muslims feel so stigmatized that they seek an "elsewhere" to flee to, like Syria or Saudi Arabia, in order to escape the persecution they suffer. In their minds, going to Syria is the only way to live peacefully.[19]

Both Saliha* and Émilie König* fit this description. Both women experienced public humiliation for wearing the niqab, which ultimately served to destroy their fragile links to society. The various laws against the veil proved to them that they are not accepted as citizens as long as they display their Islamic clothing. Such persecution gives rise to the desire for *hegira*, as Naïma S.* elaborates:

> *I'm thinking about leaving for another country, on* hegira. *My husband and I were talking about going to Tunisia. This worldly life is a prison for the believer and a paradise for the infidel. We're living proof.*

Naïma* has tried several times to leave for Syria but without success, just as she did not succeed in carrying out a knife attack on January 6, 2020, at the Austerlitz train station, even though she was prepared to do so. Émilie König,* or Ummu Tawwab in the Islamic State, was emphatic about her desire to leave in 2012:

> *I can't take it anymore. It's becoming insufferable now and I'm dreaming of going on* hegira *with my children. Once my son's health is more stable,* bi idnillah *[with God's permission] I hope to go on* hegira. *I don't really know, England or Yemen. I'd love to go to Yemen because I'm interested in prophetic medicine and I know that in Yemen they have all the plants for it [laughs].* Inshallah, bi idnillah, *I really do want to go over there.*

Although her actual destination is undetermined, she also speaks to me of her desire for revenge for all the humiliations she suffered in France. Several months later, she leaves for Syria to join a French jihadist she met on the Internet.

Saliha,* too, leaves in 2012 for Tataouine in the south of Tunisia, with hopes of reaching Syria. Each of these women went voluntarily and undertook all preparations themselves. They were neither victims of recruiters, nor were they "remote-controlled," the adjective used to describe the women who attempted the attacks near Notre Dame Cathedral in 2016. The women I met actively used the Internet to find their own contacts, and not the other way around.

Taking Radical Action

Some women choose to fight in jihad in Syria and Iraq. They adopt the rhetoric of violence, dismissing the French as "enemies of Islam." A minority of niqab wearers have chosen to respond to the law with violence and revenge, supporting the Islamic State, congratulating jihadists, and approving of their acts of violence. "ISIS is avenging us" is a phrase often uttered, marking the women who say it as jihadist sympathizers, like Naïma S.,* who states:

> I'm not surprised that there are those willing to avenge the honor of Muslim women.

Naïma* is herself driven to vengeance after her sixteen-month-old daughter is placed in the custody of social services in January of 2019. A year later, on January 6, 2020, she is arrested for an attempted knife attack at the Austerlitz train station in Paris. This radicalization, moreover, can be transmitted to children, who are often taken out of school by their mothers after the law has forbidden her access to school grounds.

In the end, the October 2010 law created what it was intended to combat: a heightened display of visible Muslim identity and the insularity of that identity. It has led to both communitarianism and also the public expression of Islamophobia, violence against women, rebellion, provocation, psychic injuries, and extremism. Alexia* laments:

> In my view it's a controversy that didn't have to happen. If they hadn't started talking about it, if they'd just left the few women wearing it alone, we wouldn't be in this state today. The niqab would've remained ignored and not many more women would have worn it.

Conclusion

The phenomenon of the niqab in the West is inextricable from modernity and the rise of individualism. It is also linked to a pre-existing tradition of facial veiling in Western societies that extends from the asceticism of Catholic orders to the extraordinary strength of superheroes, from experiences of well-being from Japan (zentai) to fetishism. Like the niqab, the Internet is a way of escaping the constraints of identity and entering a parallel world through the use of avatars that permit their user a wider moral range.[1] Multiple studies have shown the role played by social media in Salafi recruitment and radicalization. Like social media, the niqab is used to escape reality.

This desire to change one's facial appearance affects mostly women and must be linked to societal standards of beauty. This is especially true for the former beauticians, overrepresented among niqab wearers. In these women, and others, we find the co-presence of various, and sometimes contradictory, motivations for wearing the niqab. These motivations include asceticism, piety, the desire for rupture or for disappearance, exhibitionism, misandry, sensual pleasure, and the quest for the proverbial "good catch" in marriage. All these aspects and more are behind a woman's desire to wear the full veil—all except for our society's dominant cliché, which is that they have been forced by masculine coercion. The full-face veil in no way stands for a lack of self-esteem or is a sign of subordination. Far from being detrimental to its wearers, facial veiling is, for them, synonymous with power.

To veil one's face today is linked to anti-conformism; it can, for example, be a reaction to the normative, societal pressure that weighs upon an individual. In certain contexts, the niqab has quickly become a trend. Already, in traditional societies, facial veiling marked social distinction, as well as serving as the symbol of a socially superior woman with an abundance of time on her hands. It might shield from the sun, letting some women remain pale in places where tanned skin is frowned upon.

The niqab, although fetishized, is one form of bodily expression among dozens of others in a democratic society in which a need for distinction and individuation is a given for youth. Celebrated fashion designers and avant-garde artists have also used the facial veil as a cultural symbol, stripped of its religious significance, while nevertheless maintaining its controversial appeal.

At the same time, a more or less marginalized category of the population uses the veil as a means of reappropriating a strong identity and standing out via the subversive power of Islam. This use of the niqab is based on an interaction between the niqab wearer and the society she lives in: a play of attraction and repulsion that can, for some women in search of affirmation and encouraged by men who see them as the new resistance to the established order, lead to a form of infatuation. These niqab wearers, and Salafi in general, do not follow any religion in the sense of an inherited tradition. Instead, they use religion to break with societal and parental expectations.

Some women wear the niqab as a sign of their renunciation of the world and its demands on physical appearance. Whereas similar forms of feminine abnegation are accepted for Catholics and Buddhists, as well as in the cases of athletic challenges that test an individual's limits and eventually lead to a break from the world, these are denied to niqab wearers and Muslim women in general.

Niqab wearers do not always live up to their pious appearances. In some cases, their ideas of religion are cobbled together or idiosyncratic. Their religious conversations can be superficial, and their knowledge of the Quran and the Hadiths are in some cases elementary. They are uninvested in Quranic study, rarely making the effort to learn Arabic, and instead reading texts in French translation. During my exchanges with them, the religious dimension was paradoxically much less present than it was with women who wear only the headscarf. According to Olivier Roy, a majority of Salafi women access, via the niqab, an identity that appears religious but is far from a retrograde fundamentalism:

> Improvised expressions of quests for identity are systematically over-Islamized, relegating social actors to an essentialist identity, whereas they are engaged in a dynamic search for themselves.[2]

In Syria, the niqab's significance flips once again: a sign of rebellion in France, in Syria it becomes the norm. Jihadist radicalization can be sparked by extreme societal rejection: humiliations during police searches, identity checks at the police station, insults and physical aggressions from passersby in the street, not to mention the restrictions on accompanying children to school. In these cases, exterior hostility can serve as a push toward radical action.

Across this study, my work on marginal behavior allows for the confirmation of certain theories about the interaction between individuals and social context. An obsessional bias against Muslims has ultimately pushed some of them to correspond to stereotypes forged in the public opinion. Yet the juvenile excitement that we find today in some cases of Islamic radicalization might be compared to the trend in the West of Maoism during China's Cultural Revolution in the late 1960s. Salafi is an ideology that has followed Maoism, after an ideological waning of almost fifty years. The niqab in France plays a role similar to the "Mao suit," seen a half a century earlier. Both garments are the norm in their country of origin. In the West they become distinctive symbols, a way of marking out one's difference and showing one's adherence to a societally exogenous, extreme, and radical ideology.

Proponents of the ban on the full veil made use of several cultural registers, emphasizing—in spite of their purported embrace of the separation of church and state—the history of the Catholic church. The arguments against the full veil go back to Saint Paul the Apostle, superseding Moses's veil in the biblical book of Exodus, and associating the facial veil with Jews accused of blindness for not having recognized Jesus as Messiah. The slogan of the 2010 law ("The Republic lives with its face uncovered" [*"la République se vit à visage découvert"*]), makes use of explicitly Pauline phrasing.

The British scholar Maleiha Malik compares the ban to the persecution of minorities in Europe going back to the Middle Ages, between the tenth and thirteenth centuries, linking religious heretics to practicing Muslims today:

> In fact, the use (or misuse) of arguments on the subject of the autonomy of women and the equality of the sexes to justify the criminalization of the full veil suggests it: the European model of persecution has effectively evolved to the point of being dissolved in Enlightenment values such as autonomy or the equality of the sexes to better identify and persecute new victims like Muslim women.[3]

The state, in other words, has treated these niqab wearers as it formerly treated female religious eccentrics, such as Marguerite Porete, the Christian mystic condemned to be burned at the stake in 1310. Europe has a long tradition of eradicating marginalized ideologies, especially those professed by women—unconforming female mystics that the Catholic church sought to erase by condemning them as witches, to whom niqab wearers (especially converts) compare themselves regularly. Véronique,* age twenty-nine and a convert from Toulouse, who left France for Birmingham in 2012 to continue veiling, states: "It's a modern-day witch hunt and we're the witches. If they could burn us they'd burn us alive. Or throw us into dungeons." Or Sophie*: "We've been the *bêtes noires* for a long time. It's a witch hunt."

The figure of the witch has long been used to condemn independent women in Western societies. The collective condemnation of the niqab is not unrelated to the desire to erase certain women from public space: autonomous women accused of troubling the social order, as they were during the period between the fifteenth and seventeenth centuries. Today this small number of women (less than .003% of the French population) are accused, with the niqab, of damaging French national identity and even democracy itself, just as witches were formerly accused of endangering the whole of society.

Under the pretext of emancipating women (albeit against their will), the ban on facial coverings operates in a manner similar to religious tribunals, eradicating whatever part of society escapes state control and imposing uniformity. Olivier Roy also makes this comparison: "The defenders of *laïcité*," he writes, "still display traces of the Catholic inquisition."[4]

This rejection of norms represented by niqab wearers ought (ultimately) to return us to an examination of our own morals. The perpetrators of attacks against veiled women are rarely brought to justice; the victim is seen to have provoked her attacker, as often happens in cases of rape as well. In both instances, the woman is seen as guilty (in part) because of her inappropriate clothing: too revealing, too disguising. Since they have broken the law, niqab wearers are held responsible for the assaults to which they are subject. This stance is exemplary of the general, confused public attitude toward niqab wearers, held simultaneously to be victims and offenders. The case of the niqab is revelatory for Western societies that pride themselves on equality between the sexes, but still tolerate a "rape culture."[5] French society could even be schematically described as more tolerant toward rape[6] than toward the veil[7], even though the latter is worn with consent.

PART II

16 Portraits of Women Wearing the Niqab Earlier Wearers (Before 2009)

SAMIA

Algerian, Arrived in France as an Adult

Figure 3. Samia at her home in November 2009, from the film *Sous la burqa* (2010).

I meet Samia in November of 2009 on the rue Marx-Dormoy in Paris's 18th arrondissement. She is accompanied by her husband. We agree to meet again several days later at her home in the Val-de-Marne suburb, located southeast of Paris; she is excited about the idea of talking on camera. She wears eye makeup, a dark green niqab-jilbab, and stiletto-heeled boots in green suede. She is the only woman in this study who is not a French citizen, and she also represents the only example of a sexually disinhibited niqab wearer included in this book.

Profile

Born in Algeria in 1975, Samia is thirty-six years old when we first meet. She studied journalism at the university level in Algeria for three years. Her uncle was a "frérot," a member of the Islamic Salvation Front (Front Islamique du Salut, or FIS) in the early 1990s. While she was still in school, a police officer asked for her hand in marriage, but her uncle objected and threatened to kill the suitor:

> *But my fiancé was so nice—someone you could start a family with. It was a shock for me. I tried to kill myself, I was tired of living. My father was afraid to lose me, he knows what I'm worth. And then to show them I was free, I didn't care, I stopped wearing the hijab. They couldn't say a thing. I do what I want with my life—they'd have to kill me. I went out with a boy, a real whirlwind romance. But I was so young and it was a mistake, I wasn't really thinking. And actually it was to get back at my family. I wanted to punish them for having prevented my marriage—you took away my freedom, you ruined my future, I'm going to ruin yours.*
>
> *Later, I refused to marry my child's father. That's why my son now has my name. My family had to accept it, they knew that it was just getting back at them. I didn't sleep around for sex like other girls—it was to get even. After I'd been raising my son for nine years, I had the opportunity to get married to come to France. But then my husband wanted to take away my freedom. I left and notified the French police. They backed me up and helped me get to a girlfriend's house to stay for a while. Then one day I met my new husband—he's sweet, he's even-tempered, he listens to me. I've been with him for two years. I decided to wear the niqab to make him happy. I'm fine with wearing it so he knows no one's hitting on me—he's older than I am. I asked what he thought about it and he said, if you want to wear it, wear it. He lets me be as free as I want and I did it to show him my love.*

She returns to her fascination with the facial veil:

> *I always dreamed about the kind of older Algerian woman who would wear the haïk, the traditional white veil. I remember my grandmother with the 'ajar [half-veil] she put over her face. At the time, this let women go out incognito—their neighbors couldn't spy on them then. Women used to be protected from gossip and rumors. At home they wore whatever they wanted but outside they were all alike, you couldn't tell them apart. Then styles changed because of satellite TV and the taboos disappeared, women became doctors, journalists, they started to be breadwinners. But then it was bad because women were influenced by what was happening all over the world. They followed the models on TV. Then girls looked at their mothers and started hiding under the hijab again.*

Samia appears uninhibited when it comes to men and sexuality, in France as she was in Algeria:

> A neighbor came to see my mother complaining about her husband's infidelity. I exploded, I asked her, "You know why your husband cheated? When was the last time you looked at yourself in the mirror? Why don't you get a wax or wear makeup or do your hair? Go get your hair dyed, clean up a little, buy some perfume, take care of yourself and your house and your children and your husband would still see you as beautiful." She told me that her husband was visiting whores. I told her, "What do they have that you don't—a tongue, a hand? A woman can be her husband's own whore if she has to. I'm not going to teach you, turn on the TV, everyone has satellite TV here, look at what they're doing and do it." She was disgusted, she said, "That's disgusting, I'm not going to do that to him, what they're doing." I said, "So you shouldn't have married him." Then she went to my mother to tell her I was a whore. I said, "Yes I'm a whore who's teaching you how to keep your man at home. When I have a husband I'll know how to keep him. He won't go looking anywhere else. I'm going to keep my husband satisfied."
>
> I watch porn with him to satisfy us both even though Islam doesn't allow it. We just watch it to learn and then we stop, to learn what we don't know. I learned positions that helped save my sex life. It's something that makes my life better, it's good for me. I don't see any harm in it.

Disinhibited on camera, perhaps by the facial veil, she leads me into her room and lets me film her wardrobe and her lingerie:

> I dress up for my husband. I wear short skirts or shorts when there's something to celebrate, like for our anniversary. I put on a sexy dress and heels and makeup. I do my hair and we go all out. I cook, I make cakes, I do everything. I'm always ready. When I go out I'll buy sexy outfits. I wear lace, silk, thongs, slips, just about everything.

Samia kisses her son on the mouth, which tends to annoy her husband, who isn't his father. He claims to be jealous, delighting Samia. She retorts that she carried her son in her belly and that he is part of her; she affirms that she'll kiss his mouth until his marriage and then she'll let his wife take over.

She takes pleasure in showing off her freedom:

> Women are free in France. I feel protected by the law, unlike in Algeria. I never wore the niqab in Algeria. There is so much hypocrisy there—women wear it to be hidden and then go wild. For me, here, I'm not wearing it to

hide but out of respect for my husband. I want to be a free woman, I want my relationship with my husband to be good.

Often Arab women here don't like my full veil and tell me to take it off. They say: you're in France, if you want not to attract attention and not to have any problems, then don't wear it. But I'm not convinced by their arguments. Some Muslim women wear the headscarf to make people believe that they're good Muslims, but that's not what Islam is. They don't even pray. They just do it not to have to go to work and to stay at the playground with their kids, on welfare. But that's just for show too—they don't even take care of their children.

Several months later, Samia lets me know that she is in the process of divorcing and about to return to Algeria. I hear nothing else from her.

SORAYA

Parents Originally from Algeria

Figure 4. Soraya, featured in the documentary *Sous la burqa* (2010), in which she appears under the pseudonym Oum Al Kheiyr.

I meet Soraya for the first time in the fall of 2009 at the Salafi Mosque on rue Gaston-Loriaux in the Paris suburb of Montreuil. The National Assembly commission, charged with investigating the niqab, had been established several months earlier, in June of 2009. She agrees immediately to speak on camera and to be filmed going about her daily life. We are still in contact today.

Profile

Born in Belgium to parents originally from Tlemcen, Algeria, Soraya arrives in France as a child. She never reveals her age and says only that she has worn the niqab "for a very long time." She is the oldest woman in my set of interviews and the one with the highest degree of religious education. She lives alone and defines herself as independent, "a flourishing woman, comfortable with herself." She also positions herself as someone defending her rights, appealing to feminists on this count:

> *Where are all the women who struggled? Here I am, calling on them now. What right am I claiming? Well, my right to be free. It's my choice, why not give me my right to choose? As long as I'm not hurting anyone?*

She leans on verses from the Quran to justify wearing the niqab:

In surah An-Nur, in surah Al-Ahzab, God shows us how women should dress and the people she can undress before. In Quranic exegesis, you're given free will. God's texts are very clear. Women are asked to cover themselves completely—those who strive for asceticism, for perfection, even though no one will ever be perfect, that's for sure. There is always the search for good, for going beyond to please our lord. But you have the choice: if you think that it's not required, don't wear it. You can cover your whole body except for your hands and face. Or you can choose the interpretation that says: everything in a woman is beauty. The woman's first beauty is her face. If you believe that, you have to veil your face. But that doesn't mean we don't talk to people.

Soraya falls into the pietist logic of many of the first women to wear the niqab in France, or those who wore it before the 2009 controversy. In this, she is unlike the next wave of niqab wearers who tend to invoke rhetoric of protest and demand:

Some might believe that we dress this way to be noticed but it's actually the opposite. I want to become very small, I want to disappear and for no one to look at me, just to be alone in my corner. It's a desire to erase your social self in favor of your spiritual self.

Soraya evinces a certain hostility toward men. The presence of the opposite sex puts her on edge; she meets any male interlocutors with a dark look and demonstrates a general rejection of men that approaches misandry. Nevertheless, she manages at times to overcome her apprehension:

I can talk to a man and I do talk to certain men when it's clear that I have to. When I go to the hospital and there's a male doctor, I talk to him. I just ask a favor—to be seen by a woman. If that's not possible, I agree to be examined by him.

Overall, though, it is primarily women who accost her:

Once I was on the subway and a woman got on and gave me a really mean look. If her eyes had been bullets I'd be dead. She remained standing for some time, insulting me. I had just been to visit a lady in the hospital. When I got off, there were policemen outside, on the sidewalk. A woman went to them to complain. She gestured at their faces like she was saying, "That's forbidden, go talk to her, punish her or lock her up, I don't know." Before that controversy with the niqab we'd go out, run errands, go to the mosque to take classes, to try to find yourself. But since the controversy about the full-face veil, there are so many sisters I know that I don't see anymore.

In July of 2011, three months after the law takes effect, I find Soraya at home, somewhat depressed. She no longer wants to go out even to the park, which she leaves to "cruel people." Several times she claims to have renounced this terrestrial park in favor of "the celestial park that is enormously better than this one." She refuses to go with me when I propose accompanying her; she renounces sitting on the bench that is now forbidden to her, comparing the present time to the era of apartheid in South Africa.

She also declines my request to film her in 2011. She is disappointed that the law was passed and is of the opinion that her efforts on camera led to nothing. She prefers not going out at all; a "brother" does her errands for her. Suffering from a sprain, she decides to go to the emergency room wearing a surgical mask. There, no one mentions it except for a secretary who asks why she wears it and to whom she responds that it's allergies, taking out her allergy pills. "Plus it's true," she tells me, "I wasn't lying. That's how mean they are to me!" These ordeals lead her to become withdrawn. Until the passage of the law, the niqab was a means of escape for her from an unsatisfactory life. The only possibility now is to look to the afterlife.

Her disenchantment continues today, as she gives an overview of the ten years since the ban:

It's hard when something that's not harmful is banned. The niqab doesn't hurt anyone. Some women wore it to show that they were extreme—beyond reason. Lots of women have left Paris and the Paris region because of the ban. Two women I know went to Morocco, two to Algeria, maybe one to Tunisia. They went back there, just like the people who insult us wanted. Some are actually very happy. But for those who went to Syria, their life is wrecked, here and in the afterlife. Those who go there think they're doing a good thing but it's a mistake. I don't even go to the mosque anymore.

HIND AHMAS

Born in France to Moroccan Parents

Figure 5. Hind at the Institute of Islamic Culture on rue Léon in Paris's 18th Arrondissement. I filmed her version of the facts after her testimony, August 10, 2011.

Hind is thirty-two years old when we meet for the first time on August 6, 2011, in Aulnay-sous-Bois (a suburb northeast of Paris). Our encounter occurs at the Forsane Alizza rally that has been organized to protest against events that took place here one week earlier, on July 31, when Hind was arrested and handcuffed. This was one of the first police operations that had gone wrong after the ban went into effect on April 11, 2011. Hind is strong-willed and dynamic. She speaks to men naturally and confidently. She is not retiring; she does not display any of the modesty we might expect from a rigorist woman wearing the niqab.

Profile

Hind was born in France in 1979 to Moroccan parents, married in Morocco. Her father arrived in France as a worker, followed by her mother. She recounts having worn the niqab for the first time in 2005, at the age of twenty-six, at the moment she began to practice her parents' religion, which she came to on her own:

> *In my family, I wasn't given any religious education. My parents didn't teach me to pray—my friends did. I learned Islam from books. I was*

really moved by the women wearing the niqab and that became my model. Some people have Lady Gaga as a role model; my role model's the Prophet.

Alongside Kenza Drider,* who appears frequently on television, Hind confronts the ban with the support of Rachid Nekkaz. Nekkaz, a Franco-Algerian businessman and activist, organized several demonstrations accompanied by press conferences to protest the October 11, 2010 law, including one held on the eve of the law's passage at the famous brasserie Fouquet's located on the Champs-Élysées. Along with Najate Naït Ali, another woman wearing the niqab, Hind is the first woman sentenced by the police tribunal in Meaux; Hind is fined 120 euros. She has been the subject of media attention several times since then.

After our meeting in Aulnay at the Forsane Alizza rally, I suggest filming her version of the facts. We meet on the patio at the Institute of Islamic Culture in Paris on August 10, 2011. Hind is perceptibly emotional after the incident; her anger and her determination to wear the niqab are visible in her chestnut eyes. Her mindset is along the lines of "the more they want to ban it, the less I'll want to take it off."

She recounts having been led to the station in handcuffs after refusing a pat down from a police officer, attempted before even verifying her identity. Her forced handcuffing is violent and filmed; the video is widely circulated on social media. She is then contacted by Mohamed Achamlane, the Forsane Alizza leader. She agrees for the story of her incident with the police to be used by the group to help organize the rally at which Achamlane burns a copy of the penal code in public before a hundred or so Salafi individuals in religious attire.

A month later, she enjoys her victory:

I haven't been stopped again in Aulnay since I was arrested and handcuffed. When I meet police, they pretend not to see me and keep going even though now they have to know who I am. They just don't want another Forsane Alizza protest. Even in Paris I'm left alone even though I go out there almost every night. But I don't mean that women who wear the niqab don't have problems.

Over the years, however, she dissolves all links with the Forsane Alizza group, whose public burning of the penal code was largely disavowed by Muslim women:

I didn't like what they did. At no moment did they tell me they wanted to burn the penal code. They went too far. We still have to have mutual respect for the peace of everyone. The Prophet said, "If you insult their god, they'll insult yours." Mohamed Achamlane was putting on a show. They used what happened with me for advertising. So did Rachid Nekkaz, except there I was the one who got in contact with him.

In 2016, Hind no longer wears the full veil. She speaks nostalgically of her twelve niqabs and can't bring herself to get rid of them. Today she wears the jilbab:

I get tears in my eyes when I see my niqabs. When will I wear them again? I still have hope; God tests only those he loves.

She returns to the subject of the *hegira* as a consequence of Muslim women's malaise:

The hegira *is hard, you have to prepare for it. I know lots of women wearing the niqab who dream of going because they're sick of the public and police pressure. I hear about things that are so violent that I understand women who go—they push us all the way, they persecute us, to the point where we can't take it anymore. We have nothing but our minds and our bodies to defend us. In France, being Muslim has become difficult because you're judged all the time. I think of this as my country. I can't imagine leaving. And I'll practice my religion even if I get attacked for it.*

But after this mindset of being tested, she appears more disillusioned following the controversies surrounding the veil that come after, such as the attempt to ban the burqini on French beaches in the summer of 2016:

They're trying to eradicate all forms of Muslim religious display. The talk about the burqini will have an end soon, but it'll be back next year. The same thing. They want to blame all their problems on Muslims. When you listen to the French news, you can feel like the scapegoat. I don't want to ban my own living so I annoy them. They're attacking the burqini, which has nothing to do with religion. It's much too tight and revealing for us. I'm not banning myself from the beach, I swim in the jilbab and people stare at me and then come talk to me as soon as I start playing ball. At Dieppe, I was even friends with a really nice woman who sunbathed topless. Everything's coming from the media. Every woman should be able to do what she wants.

I ask Hind to reflect on the attempted gas cylinder attacks near Notre Dame Cathedral in Paris on September 4, 2016:

These women directly experienced so much hate—perhaps they were very sensitive girls. It's always like that. They wanted revenge. It is injustice that affects them. It takes me back to my past, when I was seventeen. They're careless. At that age you don't know anything about life. Of course I'm still angry, but not to the point of losing everything. Since I had my daughter, I stick with the other mothers. They're patient during these ordeals—the best thing to do here in France.

The authorities are talking about women who have been remote controlled but it's the opposite. They're so crazy that they don't know the difference between reality and a flashball shot. They're 1000% convinced. For them, we're weak and hypocritical. To me they're murderers, those little idiots. And right there in the 5th arrondissement! That's where the Paris mosque is and where I like to go out. But they were willing to kill their brothers and sisters! Even though the Prophet only allows for combat against those who fight us. It's like they're blinded. I'm not about to go blow up people who have a different religion from me!

I am still in contact with Hind, who continues to voice her desire to wear the niqab:

I want to wear it again. One day I'll leave this suburb and move to a little town or village in the country. I'll live in a house and I'll be left in peace wearing my niqab; no one will come bother me.

Figure 6. Rally organized by Forsane Alizza on August 6, 2011, held to protest Hind's handcuffing and arrest by the police a week earlier. The group's leader, Mohamed Achamlane, engages in a public burning of the penal code to mark his disapproval of the law.

KENZA DRIDER

Born in France to Moroccan Parents

Figure 7. Kenza at home in Avignon, April 11, 2013, from the film *Niqab Hors-la-loi* (2012).

I film Kenza for the first time on Thursday, September 22, 2011, during a protest in front of the courthouse in the city of Meaux, east of Paris, at which she declares her candidacy for the 2012 French presidential election. The event is staged by Rachid Nekkaz, who has rented a bus covered with posters of Kenza and slogans such as "Kenza Drider, President," "Freedom for All Women," and "I, Kenza Drider, am Running for President." On the materials handed out, she declares: "I am running in order to defend the constitutional freedom of all women in France." Or: "For all those who exercise forms of civil freedom (niqab, tattoos or piercings, even combat), it is no longer acceptable to live in fear and intolerance caused by the law which violates European rights." Numerous journalists have traveled to the event. The city of Meaux has not been chosen at random. The mayor is Jean-François Copé, the head of the center-right UMP party. Four months earlier, Kenza and Hind Ahmas* had offered him an almond cake (making reference to the fines facing niqab wearers[1]) for his birthday, three weeks after the law went into effect. Starting from the beginning of the controversy, Kenza has been active in generating media attention—taking the high-speed rail, for example, with journalists. She is dubbed the "Niqab Pasionaria" and the "Niqab Star" for having made a series of television appearances during the controversy before the law was passed. She does not hide her happiness at having advanced the cause of French niqab wearers.

Profile

Kenza was born in 1978. In 2011, she claims to have worn the niqab for thirteen years, which would mean she started wearing it in her twenties.

Both Kenza and Hind* come from modest families; both play along with their new fame. They are photographed, filmed, interviewed by journalists; their lives change completely. They find themselves at the center of the media sphere, sometimes even denigrating the journalists who close in around them.

Lila,* head of the competing organization "Amazons for Freedom," feels that Kenza and Hind appear as the opposite of Islamic decorum. According to her, the garment that signifies piety does not accord with their behavior, far removed as it is from the Islamic feminine standard. Instead of lowering their gaze before men, they joke with police officers, journalists, and their lawyer. They move freely in the masculine milieu in which they live their public lives, taking a posture at the center of such attentions that is far from the modesty incumbent on pious women:

> *They're acting like stars. It's all orchestrated by Rachid Nekkaz. They told me about going to Cannes and walking the red carpet and being photographed, like the time I ran into them at The Claridge. They were stretched out on couches and eating gyros he brought them. They were joking and saying that they were about to open some champagne—not exactly modest behavior. Nekkaz wanted me away from the association so he could keep his hold on them. He's like a rooster in his henhouse.*

The fact that certain niqab wearers have become famous—Kenza Drider and Sandrine Moulères, for example—has appeal for some women looking to escape anonymity. The niqab has in some cases become synonymous with access to fame.

Kenza receives me at her home in Avignon in March of 2013. As soon as we enter the apartment, she ushers her Belgian Sheepdog out of the living room. She introduces the dog as her fifth child, her last and smallest at a year and a half:

> *I got a dog for self-defense. When my husband is at work and I have to go somewhere on business, I'd rather go with my dog. Even if I'm flagged down in the street as* haram *[outlawed], I tell them that nothing in Islam*

forbids having a dog especially when it's for protection. And then I add: it's not like you all are about to defend me. If I'm attacked, you wouldn't lift a finger. The dog is the one who'll help me.

In the time that follows, I lose contact with Kenza.

Figure 8. Hind (left) and Kenza (right) responding to journalists' questions during the presidential campaign organized in Meaux by Rachid Nekkaz on September 22, 2011.

LILA

Born to Algerian Parents

Figure 9. Lila at home in Chambourcy, filmed multiple times in 2011 and 2012, and featured in the film *Voile Interdit* (2017).

I make contact with Lila in the spring of 2011. She has just founded an organization called "Amazons for Freedom," out of her home. She introduces herself as a trained jurist, which positions her to give free advice to women who have been fined. She lives in a well-appointed apartment in the affluent suburb of Chambourcy, west of Paris, where she has set up her telephone hotline. She stresses that she uses her own money to run the organization, and that she takes no dues from its members. She has given herself the pseudonym Lila Citar, after the sitar, the veil which accessorizes the niqab by covering the eyes. My exchanges with Lila in 2011 and 2012 are productive for the access she offers to her organization's members' complaints, as well as her accounts of the calls she receives.

"Amazons for Freedom" exists alongside the two other organizations for niqab wearers, Forsane Alizza, Mohamed Achamlane's Takfirist-leaning group, and "Citizens for Freedom," run by Kenza Drider* under the aegis of Rachid Nekkaz.

The day after Achamlane burns the penal code, Lila is livid and unequivocal:

> *Burning the penal code is an offense to the French state. Moreover, it's an act forbidden by Islam. The women fined by the police should have*

stated their identities. That would have been a good example, an opportunity to show good citizenship and obey the law.

Lila is a good source of information. For example, she is able to estimate the percentage of divorcées among niqab wearers, which she puts at 80% of her members; she attributes this high percentage to the Western way of life:

Like non-Muslims, Muslims have ended up taking marriage lightly, something that can be ended at the slightest pretext. There are no more attempts at working things out or compromise. For me this is shocking because I believe strongly in the family.

This percentage, however, needs to be put into context. She herself is not sure if the 80% of divorced women in her organization is representative of the whole of women who wear the niqab in France, or if these divorcées reach out to her because they do not have the resources to defend themselves. Lila also confirms the speed with which these Salafi women find new partners in marriage:

This speed is characteristic of our era: you meet someone, you get a religious marriage immediately and then divorce right after that. Nothing has changed when these girls come back to Islam. They flirted before, they keep on today but just in more Muslim form. They're the same kids from the suburbs, they've kept all the remains of their pasts as thugs.

Lila is quick to open up about her workdays. As her organization grows, receiving a growing volume of calls, Lila pronounces severe judgments on her members even as she counsels them in their problems with the ban and its laws. She recounts being in contact primarily with superficial women who seem indifferent about the religious obligations that come with wearing the niqab:

They don't behave like good Muslim women. I was shocked when a member revealed to me that she smokes. A niqab and a cigarette are incompatible: wearing the niqab entails a certain spiritual level, a high degree of self-control. And in Islam, it's forbidden to do harm to your body. I don't smoke myself; I don't see single men one-on-one, I'd never be seen sitting outside at a café with Rachid Nekkaz.

These are the acts she condemns in Hind* that do not match the ideal that she herself has established. Lila's vision of the niqab is a prescriptive one. She projects onto these women what she wants them to be—a model, perhaps, of herself. She elaborates different types of women in order to critique them: the "kids," minors or women in their twenties who shock her with their levity, who "want to do what the grown-ups are doing"; "women between twenty-two and twenty-eight years old, what nonsense they are, hard to find any spiritual concerns in their doings." According to her, serious women are older than twenty-eight, closer to thirty, as are the mature women Lila sees in a much more positive light. She wears and experiences her niqab in a very personal way. She does not speak Arabic and asserts her refusal to learn it, as well as to use any of the jargon with which the Salafi punctuate their speech. Despite the critiques she formulates of her members, however, she reiterates her full-time devotion for the cause she champions:

> *I take about a dozen new memberships per week and about six calls per day. Some of them are emergencies; others are to learn their rights. I intervene when women are arrested by talking to the police. This happens over the phone. Last week, a woman who was driving was pulled out of her car along with her two children. She waited at the station for four hours. She asked for a glass of water for her five-month-old and was refused. The problem is that fellow police officers never denounce such actions even if they witness them. They called her Darth Vader. These women are even threatened with being handcuffed. I had ten calls from women who called me after being arrested.*
>
> *My goal is to contest their fines. I went to the town hall. A small group of women was waiting silently for me at the exit—they had called the police. A car circled me but without doing anything. They must have recognized me. When you get stopped for a check and it's just adults it isn't a problem, but when there are children, how can you make them understand that you're not a criminal?*

Although at first Lila had thought she would be able to fight fines and to use the law to make herself heard (encouraging her members to do the same), as the weeks go by, she becomes more fatalistic. Six months after the law goes into effect, she is well acquainted with cases of excessive police force, making life for her members difficult:

> *As time goes by, I see how the police abuse their power. If you state your identity there's no reason to take you to the station and yet now that happens systematically. We could have withstood identity checks in the street, but why take us to the police station?*
>
> *Their duties are badly carried out: the police give fines in cars even though the law doesn't apply there. We are treated like delinquents or*

criminals even though we're not doing anything wrong. We are resilient: we decide to declare our identity. The law must be contested in order to show that it is discriminatory. Our only recourse is the European Court of Human Rights that guarantees our fundamental rights: to move about freely and not subject to discrimination.

Pandora's box has been opened. As soon as some individual freedoms are restricted, others will be as well. The police are taking it out on Muslim women who have done nothing to anyone; the politicians are pandering to the Front National [now National Rally].

By March of 2012, the organization has contested eight fines. Lila specifies:

Not all women who are fined appeal to the organization. Some of them pay without protest at all because they are afraid of the consequences if their names are publicized. They prefer just to settle it and be forgotten.

But Lila herself is difficult to pin down. After a period during which we speak almost daily, I break off our contact because of her authoritarian personality. Several times, she tries to take control of my work. She demands that the scenes of Forsane Alizza burning the penal code in Aubervilliers on August 6, 2011, as well as those of Kenza Drider's* presidential campaign on September 11, 2011, be removed from the documentary *Niqab Hors-la-loi* (2012). Our exchanges become so complicated that I decide to put an end to them by removing her from the final cut. After this, I lose touch with Lila; her Facebook account is no longer updated. She disappears from social media and gives no updates to the women wearing the niqab who depended on her for help.

Five years later, I include her in my documentary, *Voile interdit* (2017), since her determination is a good example of the mindset of some French niqab wearers. Her interventions allow a better understanding of the wearers of the full veil.

I try several times to contact her again, but without success. In January of 2019, a French journalist living in London tells me that she has seen her during Ramadan in 2018, in the Brixton Mosque during the breaking of the fast. According to the journalist, she still wears a black niqab with large sunglasses that cover every bit of her skin. She tells the journalist that she has moved to London with her family because she could no longer live in France, the situation having become "unlivable for practicing Muslim women." She hopes to start a new life in England.

Figure 10.

VÉRONIQUE

Convert to Islam

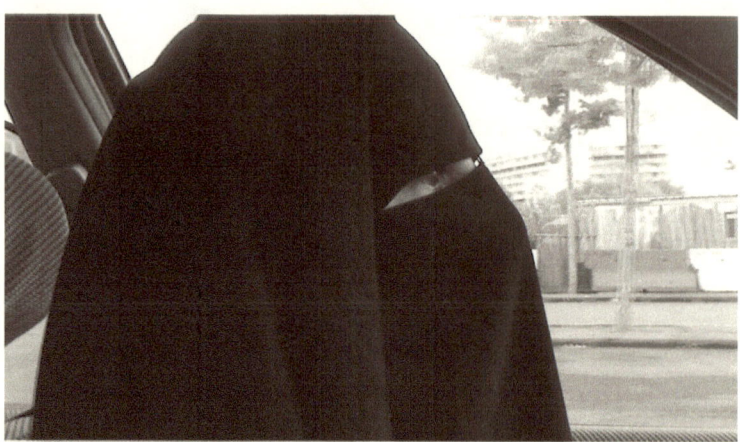

Figure 11. Véronique in the film *Niqab hors-la-loi*, under the pseudonym Stéphanie.

I met Véronique at the Basso Cambo Mosque in the Mirail neighborhood of Toulouse in 2011.

Profile

Véronique was born in 1981. A Toulouse native, she is a former beautician, now unemployed. She converted to Islam in 2004, at age twenty-four. She begins wearing the niqab after her conversion, in 2006. When she marries, she demands that her husband accept her full-face veil. She divorces in December 2010, just after the ban. Single, she decides to stop working in order to educate her daughter:

> It's been a month since I've gone out for errands. It's not so much the police who are stopping me as it is other people. I can't stand them looking at me. I don't have the courage to face being in public—I'd rather stay home.

She speaks of Forsane Alizza:

> Forsane Alizza isn't a good advertisement for Muslims. Their actions are misinterpreted by non-Muslims. I don't want to be lumped in with that.

The Prophet would never have behaved like that. That guy [Mohamed Achamlane] just wants to make himself look good in the media. That's not Islam, it's not the sunnah. *We want to calm people down and show that we're against violence.*

On November 23, 2011, she tells me that she is leaving for Birmingham in two weeks. She chooses exile in order to flee what she feels is a crackdown on the niqab; she can no longer tolerate street harassment:

I'm going to Birmingham. I have to because here all my rights aren't recognized. I'm really having a hard time. I've been asking sisters and around at the mosque. I'm going to get back into my career as a beautician and start my own business. I have no future in France. In England at least I can learn English. England isn't a Muslim country but it's better than France. I'm on my own. If one day I remarry I'll go to a Muslim country. I want to make my hegira *but that takes time.*

I don't want to marry one of the brothers here. The French brothers are frowned upon everywhere, even in Mecca. They talk the talk but they don't do anything. Especially in Toulouse—action is dead. French brothers are known for their bad behavior. And the few good ones are already taken. They don't even know the Arabic alphabet. They have no education. In England, we'll see.

After moving to a small house in a Pakistani neighborhood in Birmingham, she invites me to spend a week with her in January of 2012. She marvels at the transformation in her quality of life:

Automatically in any state office, if it's a man working there he'll call a woman to check my identity. Everyone wears the veil. Where I live it's just Pakistanis and they're sweet. The woman who lives next door is a little intrusive but I can ask her anything. I'm living again, I'm not scared of the police anymore or of getting insulted. There are a bunch of other French women who've come here because of the law. Another sister from Toulouse is here and she's really happy. Birmingham is a good alternative during the wait to go to a Muslim country. The woman in the doctor's office, even though she isn't Muslim, said she wanted to cry when I told her what was happening in France.

SOPHIE

Convert to Islam

Figure 12. Sophie near her children's school in 2016.

Sophie is one of the first women physically assaulted after the ban goes into effect. On April 19, 2011, with her thirteen-month-old son in her arms, Sophie is tackled by a woman in a zoo in Seine-et-Marne; the woman tears off her veil after reminding her of her violation of the law. With the help of her husband and son, she then pushes Sophie against a cage. All three of them admit to having attacked her, and yet it is Sophie who is fined 300 euros for her "assault." She is twenty-seven years old at the time.

Profile

Sophie was born in 1984. She speaks of having started veiling her face in July of 2008, after wearing the jilbab, and four years after her conversion to Islam at age twenty. At the time, she was working in several brasseries in Paris, which required her to take off the veil. She is one of the few married niqab wearers in my survey. Her husband is of Moroccan origin and was born in France. Her two sisters-in-law (her husband's sisters) also wear the full veil.

Sophie, who began wearing the niqab a year before the beginning of the controversy in June 2009, describes her background:

My father is an atheist and my mother is a non-practicing Catholic. I was baptized but I didn't make my first communion. I started learning about Islam in cyber-cafés: it was 2004 and there weren't very many Muslim sites at the time. In September of 2004, I went to the Paris mosque to tell them I wanted to convert. I was even wearing the veil before I converted. That's why they thought I was already Muslim. My mother was born in 1960 and she hates the niqab; she cried when I started wearing it. The day I decided to veil my face after having read about it, I said to my husband: "I'm not leaving the apartment without my niqab; go buy me one." The first time I went out wearing the niqab I felt happy. His youngest sister started wearing it six months before I did and his sister who's the same age I am started wearing it when I did. That was in July of 2008.

She recounts the assault:

I was attacked with my one-year-old baby in my arms by a couple who were fifty-five and their son who was twenty-five or thirty. I could see the license plate of their car and I filed a complaint. I couldn't travel to the court in July of 2012 because it was late in my second pregnancy, a few days before I was due. I was accused of having assaulted the man even though I was holding my child and I'm only five feet tall. They tore off my niqab and in the end I got two fines, for violence and for disorderly conduct. And yet it's written right there in the citation that I was the one who was attacked. A plainclothes policeman was there and recommended that I take down their license plate number. Then in his deposition he said that I was provoking them. Even the ones who assaulted me admitted that they started it.

People want to take justice into their own hands, especially women. Those women harass me with total impunity. Most of the time it's old, frustrated women. I feel like I'm just a punching bag for them. And yet they don't bat an eye when I'm with a man. It's all backwards. People think that we're the victims but it's us they go after.

And then I get a 300 euro fine! See, that's why I'm never going to file another complaint. Ultimately I'll always lose. My husband wants me to drop the case because he knows that the whole business is going to turn against us. That's why I'm avoiding all media attention and being so careful.

Up until 2014, Sophie remains optimistic, believing that the fines can't hurt her. But when I meet her again in January 2015, two weeks after the Charlie

Hebdo attacks, she speaks of the growing opposition that her appearance provokes:

> *Ever since the attacks, I can't leave the house. People use Charlie Hebdo as a reason to insult us. It's like we're just nothing to people, like we aren't even human. There's not a single time I go out that I don't get some kind of angry look or sign. The attacks only strengthen attacks against us.*
>
> *When I get stopped in a store, it only takes one person for the others to join in even though in more normal times they wouldn't have said anything. It's like it's contagious. All of these verbal assaults only started up after the law. Even in front of my children, they're not ashamed of insulting me. Near my children's school, I get called a bitch in front of my son by well-dressed women in their fifties. It's always the same type of women who give me trouble. But what is it that bothers them? What do I signal to these women to get them so worked up? I've never had problems with younger people. North African women can be very aggressive too, still women in their fifties. For men, the age range is bigger.*
>
> *Each social group has its own insults. Men between forty and fifty call me "bitch" or "whore"; from women, I get "Belphegor*[2] *or Batman, ghost, trash bag, raven." Both men and women use "terrorist, go back where you came from." I've never been attacked by Muslim men. And when I'm with my husband, I never get insulted.*

In November 2016, a police identity check sends her over the edge:

> *I've had enough. I'm almost ready to stop wearing the niqab. Last month I was driving my son to his Quran class. The police were behind me in an unmarked car. They demanded that I get out of the car. I lifted my niqab while getting out and suddenly they didn't know what to say. But that didn't stop them from pushing me up against the trunk of my car with my hands up to be body-searched by a woman cop. They were very violent. My daughter is four and she was in the back seat; she saw everything. They fined me for lack of visibility.*
>
> *Two weeks before that, I was in Dugny [northeast of Paris]. A cop on a motorcycle told me, "Take that thing off." I hadn't done anything. He started yelling. He told me, "Go ahead, we're following you. If you get into that car you get locked up." His tone was disrespectful.*[3] *People have no empathy for us, for them it's normal to speak to us like that. My children see me get insulted. It's hard for them. A teenager can easily react by rejecting society. Of course I don't want to ignore people who are more*

tolerant and those who come to my defense when I get stopped in the streets (even if these people are very rare). In a children's amusement park, a woman started screaming that I didn't have the right to be there because I was scaring the children. She called the management. A woman in a tank top and mini-skirt intervened. She told the woman, "You're the one who's scaring the children."

My children don't go to public school. My son was going to a Muslim school. Now I'm homeschooling them because with the niqab it's so hard to go out. I give them French lessons and my son goes to the mosque for Arabic. I like homeschooling.

But it isn't until summer 2017, more than a year later, that Sophie finally gives up veiling her face for good:

After nine years of the niqab, they finally got the better of me. For a month I was still wearing it a bit. I was never tempted to wear a surgical mask. The effect is awful, I feel sad. It's hard but it seemed inevitable to me. I'm sorry to have had to take it off but I didn't have a choice anymore. I don't feel good without the niqab—I was so used to it. But on the other hand, I feel relieved because there are fewer police stops, fewer assaults. Now I wear big glasses and I pull my jilbab over my chin.

I am still in contact with Sophie, even if she responds sporadically. She says that now she makes do with the surgical mask that has become mandatory during the COVID-19 pandemic.

STÉPHANIE

Convert to Islam

Figure 13. Stéphanie Lecuyer on the Promenade des Anglais in Nice, talking with a woman from Toulouse. From the website Franceinfo on September 15, 2016 (screen shot).[4]

Stéphanie is one of the first women to be fined under the law. I contact her for the first time over the phone in August 2011, when she is thirty-seven years old. In 2020, she still wears the niqab; she is one of the few women who has not given it up. She lives in Nice. We have not met in person.

Profile

Stéphanie was born in 1974 and converted to Islam in 1992, at the age of eighteen. Two years after her conversion, she meets her husband, with whom she has a daughter and who she divorces in 2005. She reflects on her parents and her conversion to Islam:

> *My parents are retired civil servants. My father worked at the police headquarters. That's how he found out about my conversion—when I converted the government put me on file. The police headquarters keeps documents on converts for surveillance reasons. My mother was a social services nurse.*
>
> *At the time my parents rented a student room for me so that I could study for my high school exams. I was at the library and I stumbled upon*

a Quran in French. I'll remember it for the rest of my life: I was sitting on the ground. I had a revelation, I started to cry. I felt like suddenly I understood all of humanity.

My conversion was a shock for my parents. My mother didn't understand why I chose this religion. They kicked me out even though family was very important to me. They dropped me completely—they even wanted to disinherit me. I slept on the street and then I got an apartment through social services and could continue my studies. God gave everything back to me. The break with my parents lasted for a year. When they saw that I was managing alone they got back in contact, and then five years after me they converted to Islam. But my father has trouble with my niqab, and besides he never liked my husband. I hid my divorce from him for five years because I thought he would hold it against all Arabs.

When I saw Mecca on TV, I cried when I saw the women. They were magnificent. Then I said the salat al-istikhara [prayer for advice] for a year. Every three months, I had a confirmation dream. I was praying to Allah to be able to wear the niqab all my life. And Allah said yes. I made my first niqab myself by sewing together pieces of black cloth. Now I wear colors. I bought my colored niqabs in Egypt. Here the stores don't sell them anymore because the law bans it.

Today my niqab is like my underwear: I can't go without it. I like it, for me it's good and pure. Before I was unbalanced but the niqab has calmed me. I got my drivers license wearing my niqab. I got my contract as a nursery school assistant wearing my niqab. But when the ban was passed, I could only cry.

Stéphanie is one of the few women in my study who has studied religion and Arabic. She completed two years of legal studies at the Sorbonne and a degree in theology from a private Islamic college. She spent two years in Egypt studying Arabic and then time in Morocco, the country of origin of her daughter's father, where she taught preschool. Upon returning to France, she got a degree in early childhood education to become a preschool assistant. For her student teaching in a public school, she was required to take off her niqab to go in, although she was able to wear her hijab. After that student teaching, she does not work but is still seeking occupation:

I always wanted to work so as not to be criticized: I don't want it to be said that women who wear the niqab live off of others. I was shocked by some younger women who use the niqab as an excuse to do nothing. Many young sisters wear the full veil and don't work, they don't want to live in society. But for me, for my training, I agreed to make compromises, in other words to take off my niqab when I went into the daycare. But I put it back on when I leave work. I want to become a professional. I don't have a choice.

She returns to the reasons for her divorce:

I'm the one who wanted a civil marriage, it was very important for me and for my family. Everything was good but after ten years I met my in-laws. Their customs killed me. They never appreciated me for myself. My in-laws couldn't stand my niqab. I brought them flowers that went straight into the trash. I was supposed to have brought cakes, very fancy ones, but I didn't know anything about that. All I could bring them was religion. But for them, the only thing that counts is money, money, money.

They came to visit us in France. They saw that I ate sitting on the ground, that I slept on the ground, and they couldn't accept it. It's true that there isn't the level of comfort that they have, but I do what I want in my own home. I came to them all "peace" and "love," I was naïve and non-suspecting, but they rejected me completely. We divorced in 2005.

I can talk about it now but before I couldn't stop crying. Maybe I'll reunite with my husband in janna [paradise]. Now I'm able to tell myself: may God pardon them. As for me, I picked myself up fast—God is my therapist. I don't need antidepressants. If I had to live with my daughter's father again, we'd only have a religious marriage. I'd be considered only his concubine in the eyes of the state but I don't care.

On August 27, 2011, Stéphanie is stopped by the police three times in one day. She recounts having cried that evening:

For me, my life is reduced to necessity. If I go out it's because I have to, for my daughter. I have to live. Anything can happen when you go out. I put my life in God's hands. I have plans, so much professional ambition. In the Prophet's day women were important in business, they were the important teachers. I don't think of myself as a victim. Like Edith Piaf says, "Je ne regrette rien."

I don't claim to be Salafi or Tablighi, I just want to live according to the sunnah. *I can't stand the men who say that a woman can't travel without her* mahram. *I ask them what they think of divorced women who don't want to get remarried. Islam isn't a kind of etiquette—it's a simple thing. In order to protect myself I have to stay in my corner, just surviving.*

> *The women who are part of those groups don't make any compromises, or else they just stay home. A sister who was going to nursing school stopped because she didn't want to compromise. That, I don't understand.*
>
> *Now you see new Muslim women, sixteen-year-old girls wearing the niqab who go out in town. I am saddened by this new wave that comes after me, these sisters belong to these groups and they don't study, they don't even know Arabic. I have my degree in theology. They're lost—some of them are on their fourth marriages. Sometimes the women haven't decided to wear it on their own but out of a desire for closeness with their husbands. When their passion wanes, they'll drop it.*

Since the beginning of their public stigmatization, the majority of niqab wearers seek dialogue. Stéphanie was filmed during a verbal exchange with a female French tourist in Nice in September of 2016. She was the subject of a journalist's reporting from the Promenade des Anglais in Nice after the attacks in Nice on July 14, 2016.

In May of 2020, Stéphanie affirms that she still wears the niqab in public:

> *I am still passionate about the niqab. Certainly there have to be rules for safety and identification, but we should be able to wear it in the street or in a shop. Now I refuse to do interviews. And yet as a woman I'd like to speak in public, I have a feminist side. But the journalists we face just want to categorize us as Salafi. That's why I don't talk about religion with people anymore; it doesn't do any good. I talk about freedom of conscience but not religion. And to me they talk about freedom of opinion but they don't actually respect it.*

Neo-Niqab Wearers (After 2009)

ALEXIA

Convert to Islam

Figure 14. Alexia (Cindy) in the documentary *Niqab hors-la-loi* (2012).

I meet Alexia for the first time during the Forsane Alizza rally in Aulnay-sous-Bois on August 6, 2011. The group is protesting the arrest and handcuffing of Hind Ahmas,* and Alexia is thirty-six years old at the time. I approach her when she is standing apart, wearing a sitar. She is an active member of Forsane Alizza and the religious wife of the group's spokesman. This is the beginning of a research relationship that continues today. I witnessed her spectacular evolution from stubborn Takfirism and a deeply felt commitment to wearing the niqab, to the gradual abandonment of the veil and her exit from Islam, and then, finally, her entry into Spiritism; now she frequents the Allan Kardec Center in Paris. She is the niqab wearer that I know best; I have had access to each part of her life for the past ten years. In January 2018, I served as witness for her marriage at the town hall.

Profile

Alexia[5] was born into a middle-class family:

> I grew up in a detached house in the Val d'Oise department north of Paris, in a little town away from housing projects and thugs. I got my beautician license at age sixteen. A nude woman in an ad isn't shocking to me because I grew up with that. I dyed my hair and wore makeup starting at age thirteen, which is when I became a fan of brand-name perfumes. I was attracted by everything superficial, physical. My mother wasn't like that at all; she had only ever been with my father and she always wore suits. I'm the only person in my family who was like that. I was raised atheist, with a hatred of religion.

Alexia has a promiscuous past marked by multiple sexual liaisons. Very early on she confides in me about her relationships with men:

> I started early and sometimes I had as many as ten boyfriends at a time. A friend kissed me on the mouth when I was thirteen. I wasn't attracted by sex but by seduction. I could get whatever I wanted from men. It always ended badly. I was always the one who dumped my partners, because I wasn't satisfied. When I was young, I'd go to nightclubs and chase guys.

She becomes pregnant for the first time at age eighteen by a man who is not the man she is living with at the time. Her mother forces her to have an abortion. Shortly after, she falls in love with a man she meets at a bar who has a criminal history and has just been given a long sentence for violence. She lives with another man while still flirting in the visiting room with the detainee who will become the father of her first two sons. Her conversion to Islam at age twenty-two ends her period of promiscuity:

> Islam is what stopped me flirting with ten men at a time. If I hadn't had the barrier of religion, I would have gone from one man to another until I found the perfect guy.

Her Conversion

> I was a beautician when I converted. At the time I couldn't even have imagined going out without makeup. My dream was drag queens. I was with a Kabyle who didn't care at all about religion. A neighbor gave him the film "The Message," with Anthony Quinn, recounting the origins of Islam. I wanted to see it because I liked costume dramas. I kept thinking about it all night. Allah had called me! The next day I went to buy my

first books and I prayed. I stopped being a beautician since it's impossible to be veiled and dressed super fashionably at the same time.

The Niqab

It was in July of 2009, and my youngest son was a year old. The mayor of Vénissieux [André Gerin] started the controversy. He's the one who inspired me to do some Internet research. One evening I saw a sister interviewed on the channel France2. She was only nineteen but she seemed so poised! It didn't take me long to be convinced of the obligation to cover the face. The scholar Ibn Uthaymin said: if a woman should cover her feet, then what does that mean for her face? Such logic! I still think about that phrase—the lightbulb moment and then in two weeks I knew I had to wear the niqab. I went to the rue Jean-Pierre Timbaud off the Couronnes metro stop in Paris to buy my first sitar, which covers the eyes as well as the face. The full veil boosts both a woman's confidence and her beauty.

If the Vénissieux mayor hadn't launched the fact-finding commission, I would never have worn the niqab. He was sent by Allah. These politicians got caught in their own trap. I completely renounce their republic, their democracy, their government, and their separation of church and state. They can have their religion and we'll have ours.

Lots of my friends and family didn't understand when I started wearing the niqab. They saw it as a kind of imprisonment, like its own form of marginalization. The truth is they can't tolerate difference, or the fact that I'm not like them.

I didn't know God as a teenager, I discovered Him as a young adult. I wanted to make up for lost time. I wanted to do more to please God and to strengthen my bond with Him.

After February 29, 2012, active Forsane Alizza members' accounts were frozen for "incitation to armed violence" by the Minister of the Interior, Claude Guéant. Following the group's dissolution, Alexia looks back on her path:

I joined Forsane in January of 2011. They were the only ones condemning the law banning the niqab and fighting injustice. I was seduced by them. I felt fully recognized. I was active on their website and I wrote several articles. I went to their rallies. It was not only at the demonstration in Aulnay where Cortex burned the penal code. We gathered on other occasions too with Sharia4Belgium and Sharia4UK. At the beginning, Forsane was a united group with strong fraternal links. I left in September of 2011, after six months. The group had changed a lot. The new recruits were vulgar people, Cortex [Mohamed Achamlane's nickname] would let anyone in. He asked the members to pledge allegiance to him and to think of him as their emir. We saw him on videochat. He was raving. Many members felt trapped and they couldn't quit because of their vows of allegiance, out of fear of disobeying God. Cortex was straying. I didn't feel at home there anymore and I chose to leave.

The reporting on Forsane Alizza made the group seem ridiculous.[6] When I saw it I told them: "You look like clowns." I had already left. Lots of members distanced themselves from Cortex after the reporting. He wasn't mean, despite his outsized ego. But in the end he was doing stupid things. The members were ignorant. Going after Forsane is like going after a bunch of clowns.

On May 1, 2012, I put Alexia in contact with Saliha.* This is the first time the two have met, even though both were members of Forsane Alizza. After their first exchanges, their conversation turns to men. Each one had entered and ended four Muslim marriages. They assert that they both had chosen to separate after marital violence. Both agree that they are very demanding in their choice of husbands.

They also admit a penchant for men that they describe as irresistible and difficult to reign in. Alexia speaks of her insatiable appetite:

I'm always trying to attract men. I wear the niqab only because it's a religious requirement. Otherwise I'm awful about men. Even as a Muslim, I want men to look at me.

Saliha agrees, adding that since converting to Islam, she makes herself lower her gaze when she meets a handsome man in public, whereas previously she tended to stare at him. She says she has used the sitar, which hides the eyes as well, to cast furtive glances at men. She confesses to her desires as a kind of "adultery with the eyes." Alexia, though, says that she doesn't like looking at a handsome man so much as being looked at by him. She explains the type of relationship she looks for:

I'm not submissive. I'm very possessive in love, and very dominating. I need a man with a strong personality who can possess me. A man can possess me but not dominate me. One day I went to a therapist who told me, "You're very authoritarian. More than just dominating men, you

want to crush them." It's true that I'm super possessive. If all women
covered their faces, then my man wouldn't be able to see any of them.
There would be no problems with infidelity.

Even though she can't understand the public intolerance about her dress, she reasserts her disgust at mixing with people. This attitude differs greatly from Émilie's*: the latter seeks good relationships with others, especially with her neighbors.

Alexia defines herself as a Takfirist, opposed to the *taghut*, or the state and its institutions:

All Muslims who try to compromise with society are engaging in chirk *[polytheism]. You have to separate from the* taghut. *To get married at the town hall, to hire a lawyer, I refuse all of that. The police are* taghut *pawns. On one hand Cortex wanted to leave behind the* taghut *but on the other he hired lawyers to defend him with* taghut *laws! It makes no sense. But it's not a problem to take money from the state, that's a right, that's money they owe you. It has nothing to do with the* taghut *to which I will never pledge allegiance.*

Ibn Baz and Ibn Uthaymin, the men we call the "palace scholars" for their association with the Saudi regime, represent the pinnacle of taghut, *they're turncoats who issue fatwas against the fundamentals of Islam to protect their rulers. These men aren't Muslim; sharia doesn't apply in their countries. Those scholars have broken the truth, they've turned Muslims into infidels.*

The problem with the Salafi [pietists] is that they follow the palace scholars, they don't practice Takfir *towards infidels and bad Muslims. They can't call themselves Muslims. We call them the* talifi *[literally, "those who lead people astray"], or the pseudo-Salafi.*

I define myself as a ghulat *[extremist], I am extreme, I criticize bad Muslims. We're on the quest for perfection. For the* ghulat, *the whole world is infidel unless you can prove the contrary. The intention is good. The* ghulat *are takfiri, but we aren't jihadists. For them, jihad just means to plant the* tawhid *flag. Jihadists can also be takfiri. ISIS is the peak that can be found: jihadists and* ghulat, *both. But for me they're not jihadists, they're killers. Qital is armed combat. ISIS are not qitalists. It's not only ISIS in Syria and Iraq, there are lots of other* mujahidin. *Besides some groups have been the first to denounce ISIS.*

She enters into a relationship with a man she meets on social media. A convert to Islam, he is fourteen years younger than she is and lives with his mother in Normandy. He proves to be strongly influenced by the situation in Syria and sympathetic to jihad. Their union is very short, but she keeps in regular contact with him:

> *My last ex-husband told me about the Dawla* (ad-Dawla al-Islāmiyya fi al-'Irāq wa-š-Šhām, *the Islamic State in Iraq and the Levant, which gave its name to the French acronym Daech). He made it clear that he wanted to go to Syria. He was in contact with people in the Dawla. It was a group that wasn't known at the time. There were many groups and the Dawla was one of the bloodiest that would fight you if you didn't give them your allegiance.*
>
> *He wanted to go to Syria to join them. He was met by his contacts at the airport in Istanbul. He went into debt for it and he bought four thousand euros worth of computers and perfume and various supplies for them. They took him out to a restaurant after they put him up in a hotel, promising to take him over the border the next day. But when he got back to his room, his bag was empty and all the cash, all the stuff he had brought, all of it was gone. So from being the one who wanted to rip off the bank, he's the one who got ripped off. He had to come back to France and he'll have to pay it back.*

In August of 2014, when she has stopped wearing the niqab, I ask her about her former belief in *ghulat* thought:

> *I probably became* ghulat *because I felt superior, I couldn't tolerate men and women who didn't conform, women who wouldn't veil their faces. I had a tendency to put down others, I saw them as inferior beings and I was sure all that was perfectly in line with God. When I wore the niqab I didn't feel inferior despite what the feminists say. No one forced me. It was only later that I realized I had been manipulated and I stopped wearing it. But that doesn't mean the pseudo-feminists who attack the niqab are right, because it was my choice to wear it. They think they want what's best for women but they're dragging us down, they destroy us, they're persecuting us. I got out of it but not thanks to them.*
>
> *The problem with the* ghulat *is that everything was subject to debate. If you don't practice* takfir *against this or that then you're an infidel. You become Muslim when you follow their dogma. They even think it's allowed to steal in Muslim bookstores. This branch of* ghulat *is a complete other religion. My ex-husband was like that, he practiced* takfir *because he was after perfection, he went over to the jihadists. He kowtowed to ISIS, like Samra [Émilie König*].*

I ask for her reaction to the recent self-proclamation by Abou Bakr al-Baghdadi (1971–2019) as the caliph of the Islamic State on June 29, 2014, the first day of Ramadan:

> When Baghdadi preached two months ago, it's true that he was a charismatic presence. But he's a fake. Those people kill Muslims, they're imposters. You have to have a bloodthirsty side to go to Syria. Forsane Alizza, on the other hand, has an innocent side, nothing to do with jihad. They're people who aren't dangerous at all, theirs is a harmless strain of thought. There's a huge difference between joining Forsane and enlisting in ISIS. What tore us apart at the time was the birth of ISIS, of Dawla, of the Islamic State. Before, we were just divided on Facebook. Now everyone's gone their own way.
>
> In Forsane, there was a debate that started in an online meeting. Some members were for suicide bombings. We were all chatting before Cortex came, because he was against it. Some people were justifying the attacks. Opinion was equally divided. Selma was one of the first members to go to Syria and also one of the first members of Forsane; she was very aggressive. She was the one who called for people to go there. Some members were fans of the Ansar al Haqq website, which is now gone. I had downloaded lots of texts that justified murder and jihad.
>
> The men and women who went to Syria had problems with their behavior and their common sense. They were thugs, and when those kinds of people encounter Islam they take a part of it and they drop the rest. They'd been in prison and they'd become shady. They'd been taught things that made them hateful, especially since they were already really quick to anger. But for me, I wasn't at all interested in jihad. In my group we got called hypocrites by the pro-jihad faction—"sheep," "French Islam." The same terms we used for the takfir got used against us.

Alexia Gives Up the Niqab in Fall 2014

> The first time I went out with my face uncovered, I felt like I was emerging from prison or from a depression. I felt the ocean air even though I live in Seine-Saint-Denis, that's how fresh it felt. I got used to it quickly but there are still some after-effects that I have trouble getting over. It took years to get out of it and I still haven't finished cleaning out some things mentally. My anxiety attacks are still here. For five years I was oppressed. I was cut off from the world except for the Internet, it was a tool for spreading hate. I've become more tolerant now that I'm not

> wearing the niqab and I've started being with people again. That's the moment when I started living again.
>
> It wasn't the harassment that made me give up the niqab, or the arguments by politicians and feminists, but my ex-husband who thought I should take it off when he saw my physical state. It was even more surprising from him because he thought the niqab was required.
>
> That law that was supposed to free women has done the opposite. It has ostracized us, it's kicked us out of society. For me, it caused psychological damage because I was afraid to go out, it was repressive. In no way did it free women. The majority of us are mothers or single women. For five years I fought the cops, the government, people in the streets. It was combat every day and it made me sick. I was alone. They wanted to make the niqab disappear but instead they have multiplied it. I'm against the laws that ban the veil, because each one of these laws causes harm to the freedom to exist, it makes women unhappy. A ban is violent, especially when women believe they're pleasing God. It must not be banned.
>
> Now with distance, I realize that it was a mistake to burn the penal code. I can put myself in other people's shoes. Of course they had a negative image of Cortex's actions. Besides, nothing changed. The 2010 law against the full-face veil wasn't revoked. Islamophobia is still mounting. I think it should have been done differently.

As time passes, Alexia becomes increasingly severe toward the niqab. In January 2016, a year and a half after she stops wearing it, she affirms:

> No, I wasn't really into the niqab. You know how excessive I was. If I hadn't believed it was for Allah I would have never have worn it because I love attractiveness so much. I don't believe the women who say that they wear the full veil to be protected from the male gaze. It's impossible. As women, we like to be seen.

Each time I visit her at home, Alexia returns to that period of her life, blaming the theological system:

> For me, the doctrine of imprisoning a woman is abusive. This Saudi Islam goes against what's good for women. They circulate texts that make women believe it's for their own good. Actually, you do feel good in a rigorist sense since you think you're going to please God. You're so deeply inside it, in a whole other logic. But once you start thinking for yourself and you understand that it's manipulative, a fraudulent use of religion, then everything becomes clear. It's a sneaky form of domination

to subjugate us. I blame both Saudi Arabia and French law. The one imprisoned me and the other hunted and persecuted me.

In August 2017, Alexia meets a man on Facebook. She introduces him as a former soldier and freemason, or in other words everything she hated during her *ghulat* period. She compares their radical opposition to an alliance between a Nazi and a Jew. On October 27, she asks me to be the witness for her marriage, which will take place three months later at the city hall, another transgression of her former ideology. She sums it up:

I covered myself for nineteen years. After the niqab, I wore the veil for three years. For me today, religion is much less important. What's important is my relationship with God, which I find now in certain rooms in the Louvre. In my new job, I'm undercover. No one knows I'm Muslim, I listen to what my colleagues say and I begin to understand people who are Islamophobic. I understand that Muslims want to exist with their own identity. But as long as Muslims have a bad image, it's better to keep a low profile.

In 2018, Alexia starts going to the Allan Kardec Center in Paris, where she attempts to communicate with spirits. She invites me several times but, becoming discouraged after not being able to contact her deceased grandmother, she turns toward shamanism. I let her know when Mohamed Achamlane (sentenced to nine years in prison) is freed on January 1, 2020. She responds tersely, "I forget whoever I'm not interested in."

Figure 15. Two former Forsane Alizza members: Alexia, right, meeting Saliha, left, for the first time on May 1, 2012.

HANANE

Parents of Algerian Origin, Convert to Islam

Figure 16. Hanane (Zouleykha) in the documentary *Niqab hors-la-loi* (2012).

Hanane was born in 1990 in the suburb of Créteil, southeast of Paris. I meet her for the first time in January 2010 during the "Free Women's Protest," which begins in the Place de la République in Paris and moves southwest toward the National Assembly. This small group of women has gathered to protest the ban on facial coverings, which would be passed ten months later. Hanane is nineteen years old at the time, and asserting her right to wear the niqab, which she began wearing a month earlier, in December 2009. For her, wearing the niqab is a way to emulate the Prophet's wives. She also describes the feeling of well-being that comes with veiling her face: "I feel better than when I'm not wearing it. Without the niqab, I feel like I'm naked."

In March of 2012, she takes stock of her everyday existence:

I've been wearing the niqab for two and a half years. I have fewer problems with the police than with people who insult me—they're always shouting "Go back to your own country," etc. People are crazier than the police. A guy sat down beside me in the subway and he wouldn't stop staring at me. I got off, he got off. I was afraid, I was wondering what he wanted.

I run into her by chance on the Rue Jean-Pierre Timbaud in Paris in 2014. She is still wearing the full veil and has gotten married. She recounts having succeeded in convincing her husband to tolerate it: "I was wearing it already, there was nothing he could say." She has just quit her job as a telephone operator, for which she was forced to lift her niqab.

In April 2016, she contacts me again after having disappeared, shutting off her cell phone and her email. Now she is twenty-five years old and describes herself as self-employed:

> *I stopped wearing the niqab a few months ago. It wasn't livable anymore. It got too dangerous. I had to stay home. The women I know who still wear it aren't doing anything in life. They're shut in, cut off from the world. They homeschool. On the one hand, the law worked, because they're afraid of going out and they stay home, so they aren't seen anymore in public. But actually it hasn't worked at all, because there are more of them even if they've lost all freedom. I agreed to take off the niqab in institutions but not in public. If the law was revoked I'd wear it again but little by little, because I'm afraid of being insulted.*

She asks me to help her write a book about her life. She wants to tell her story of being sexually abused as a child (now a closed case) and to make her experience public:

> *What I want is to give hope to women who were raped. I was raped when I was around four, five, six years old. It ended when I was fourteen and went into foster care. I was raped by my uncle and my stepfather. When my mother found out she wanted to play it down because she thought it was just touching. She was very abusive.*
>
> *I met my father when I was fifteen. He didn't care about me at all. When he learned what my stepfather had done, he didn't react at all. One day, I went to school with my head cut open from my mother and stepfather. My teacher sent me to see the social worker and that's how I got put in foster care when I was fourteen. My lawyer said I could bring him down but I dropped the case because I couldn't stand going to court with my mother, who was accusing me of having been her husband's mistress. That lasted for four years. At the time I was so upset with them. I tried to commit suicide multiple times. But after my conversion when I was nineteen, I stopped being mad at them. I told myself, there's a God, God will take care of it. My vengeance is that I got out of it. Even with Algerian parents, I had to convert to Islam because they weren't practicing.*
>
> *At the group home there were lots of girls in similar situations who ended up in mental institutions. I got through it thanks to the niqab. The state's done nothing for me and that made me want to wear it even*

more. I went from one home to another. In the book, I want to speak about my path from childhood to now, all the steps I went through. I want to show women who have been raped that they can get through it.

Hanane and Men

I started wearing the niqab after getting into religion when I was nineteen and a half. The niqab occurred to me because I don't like men. I want to hide from them. I could see them but they didn't see me. I felt good wearing it. Now when guys look at me when I'm not wearing the niqab it annoys me. But I don't see myself putting it on again; it's too dangerous.

At first I didn't know what religion to choose, Christianity or Islam. I chose Islam because it's the fairest and most rational religion. I watched videos on YouTube. A Tablighi man who came from Villiers, near the home, told me lots about religion. My first husband was Tablighi. I went twice on the women's khourouj. Even if Tablighi helped me get through it, today I think only Salafi is the true religion. Lots of Salafi girls came to it from Tablighi. I got pregnant and I had a miscarriage. We stayed together for a year and a half. My second husband was an Imam. He was also Tablighi but didn't tell me. Then I met my co-wife on Facebook. We both had the same husband. We'd married him a month apart. She was mad!

My new husband is Salafi, an electrician. After our marriage, he made lightning progress in religion. He thought there was too much music and too much mixing of the genders in France and that's why he didn't want to go out anymore. I told him that I was going out whenever I want. I go out a lot with my girlfriends, bowling or to restaurants, walking on the Champs-Élysées. I need to move—otherwise I think too much about the past. He tells me he doesn't want to go out because he's afraid of falling back into it. I'm not in love with him. We're just in a religious marriage. On Sunday it was nice out, I suggested we go boating in Vincennes. He said no so then I called someone else, my lover. He came straight there and we strolled around. We stayed out at a restaurant until 2 A.M. I haven't gone out with my husband for three years. It's the only thing I want from him. He's in love, but I'm not. That's what pushed me to have a lover. I love him a lot. I'd rather have a lover than leave my husband and hurt him. I put others before myself. I'm talking to you because you're an older woman and can give me advice.

I've been married three times, with Black men each time. I like Black men. My current husband is Senegalese. I met my lover in a hookah bar.

> He's Congolese but he's Christian so that's out. I want to raise my children in Islam. He's just keeping me company. I haven't had sex with him. That night we fell asleep together. I want to take my time because I don't want to sleep with him and then not hear from him anymore. It's going well like this. I don't want to get with an Arab. Impossible. I'm not generalizing but I have trouble with Arabs, I think because my stepfather is Algerian.

Hayat Boumeddiene

Hanane recounts having been well acquainted with Hayat Boumeddiene, the wife of Amedy Coulibaly, who carried out the attacks on the Hyper Cacher supermarket at the Porte de Vincennes on January 9, 2015:

> Hayat and I went to middle school together. I heard from her three weeks before her husband Amedy Coulibaly's actions. She invited us for a meal and she was all worked up, encouraging us to go to war. Her husband was the one who had convinced her. Earlier she was totally normal. She was wearing the niqab two years before the law. She was one of the sisters in my group of friends. We all wore the niqab and would organize dinners with the sisters. She was also in Villiers-sur-Marne like me when I was in the home.
>
> She'd been with Amedy for a long time. He was cool until he was in jail. When he got out, it all went nuts. I don't know why he was in jail but it was for something small. Hayat wanted to set me up with a man to marry; she was very insistent. The guy had been in prison for a murder in a brawl. It's good that I didn't marry him or else today I'd be in Syria [laughs]. Then the girls stopped coming to the meals. At first it was nice to be with them but in the end she got old. She was telling us to take up arms, to go to war. I stopped going.

Hanane calls me in September 2017 to tell me that she has stopped wearing the veil:

> That's it, I'm divorced. My ex-husband had fertility problems. I wasn't in love with him. Now I don't wear anything on my head. I took it all off because I live alone and I work. I'll definitely wear the niqab when I'm married. Today it's going fine without it but one day I'll get married again and of course I want to wear it again. I feel good wearing it. I'll do it for God and for my husband.

We meet in November 2017 in the Starbucks in Paris's Place d'Odéon. She has come to the neighborhood to visit the Aromazone store, which sells natural cosmetic bases with which she wants to start an online store. She asks me to make her business cards and labels for her bottles: avocado oil, aloe vera oil, mascara with castor oil, a hair mask. I make a logo for her new business. She returns to her decision to stop wearing the niqab:

> *As I got farther along in religion, I wore the niqab without ever having seen it as required. Religion brought me a lot and the more I went on the more I wanted to be covered. I found advice in books, audio recordings, on the Internet. I was nineteen or twenty when I started wearing the niqab and twenty-five when I took it off. Today I hardly ever pray on time and there are even days when I don't pray. When I wore the niqab, I was more regular about it but still sometimes I prayed late.*

I lose contact with Hanane at the end of 2018. She stops calling me for her labels or for help with her book. The Facebook account where she lists her products is no longer updated.

Figure 17. Hanane (second from right) during the "Free Women's Protest," organized spontaneously by niqab wearers and other women wearing the veil in January 2010.

SALIHA

Convert to Islam

Figure 18. Saliha in 2012, just before her departure for Tataouine, Tunisia.

I meet Saliha for the first time on April 7, 2012, on the street not far from Paris's Gare du Nord train station, a year after the law goes into effect (April 11, 2011). She was stopped the previous evening for wearing a surgical mask (not the niqab) and taken to the police station. She lives in a quiet town in the Seine-Saint-Denis suburbs of Paris.

Profile

Saliha is of Martinican origin. A single mother, she is a laundry worker in a retirement home. She recounts the process of her conversion to Islam:

> *I converted when I was nineteen years old. It was just after September 11. I was in high school completing my vocational degree. The first year of that I was pregnant, the second I had my son, and a year after that I converted to Islam.*
>
> *What sparked my conversion was the birth of my son. A female cousin had converted to Islam and my mother to evangelism. So I had the examples. I didn't go straight to Islam. I compared the two religions. I showed my mother a verse in the Bible where it says that pork is forbidden.*

Her response was, yes but still. She didn't give any convincing explanation, whereas in the Torah it's forbidden and so in the Quran too, they're in agreement. The vast majority of Christians don't follow God's commandments. Muslims are the only ones who take the Quran literally, or at least we try.

I stayed in school despite everything. I passed my professional exams in arts and crafts, in sewing. My professors tried to understand the reasons I converted. It was a personal process. I started wearing the veil little by little: first the hijab, then the jilbab in 2008, and then the niqab just when it was banned. It's a myth that husbands force their wives to be covered. I'm not married, I'm a single mother.

My son's father was North African. People always wanted to know if I converted for him and I said no, he wasn't the reason I converted. People have to stop thinking that it's the man who makes the woman convert and wear the veil. It's like we're incapable of thinking for ourselves and so there has to be a man behind us deciding for us to wear the veil—it has to stop! Often women want to wear the full veil and it's the men who won't let them, even threatening to divorce them.

She invites me several times to her house. She is at ease speaking on camera and addresses an imaginary public, using the occasion to settle the score:

What's bizarre is that I've been stopped wearing a surgical mask but not wearing the niqab. The surgical mask isn't a problem except when it's associated with a jilbab, or in other words a Muslim woman. If the police try to check my identity, I'm not going to raise my veil. I'll go to the station to get identified by a woman in private. But I refuse in front of men. I'll lose four hours of my time but it doesn't bother me. I'm sticking with the niqab no matter what happens. That's that.

I walked past a woman who called me Belphegor. They must have small vocabularies because it's Belphegor, Belphegor, every time. Ok fine, I'm Belphegor. That's just fine by me.

The law is hard to implement. There's still a law in effect that says women can't wear pants. I keep a record of this law in my bag, so if the bus driver says anything to me I'm going to take it out and shove it in his face and show it to him: if you won't let me get on this bus, then you can't let any women wearing pants on either. That ban is still in effect.

Some niqab wearers make use of this French law concerning women's clothing after Mohamed Achamlane called attention to it. The law in question was an 1800 ruling from the Paris prefect forbidding "women from cross-dressing," or wearing pants, to prevent them from participating in careers reserved for men. Women could only wear pants on doctor's orders or to ride a horse or bike. After two centuries, the prohibition was lifted on February 6, 2013.

Love of the Niqab

I've always liked the niqab. It's a love that I've had starting from when I converted to Islam. But at first I didn't dare. The law pushed me to start doing some research. I believed and so I started wearing it. It's a religious obligation, of course, but now the niqab also represents resistance for me, resistance to the illegal law that deprives me from the freedom of dressing the way I want, of practicing my religion the way I want.

Before the law, I practiced Islam simply—I said my prayers and fasted. But now when I go out it's like I'm making jihad, in other words I know I'm going to get insulted. The hate is climbing day after day with this law. And it's us women who are attacked first. Honestly, the more they stare at me and the more they insult me, the stronger my faith grows. The niqab represents resistance, resistance to the oppression we face every day. With each controversy surrounding the veil or Islam we get insulted and harassed because the veil we wear represents Islam. I don't see myself taking it off; I'm holding on to it.

At first, I didn't want to wear it right away. I wore a surgical mask instead to divert some of the stares. But as things went along I couldn't stand the mask, it was stifling. What made up my mind was when I got stopped because I was wearing a surgical mask. With the niqab it's easier to breathe.

Actually, I thank M. Sarkozy and M. Guéant for having started the controversy. Without it I wouldn't be wearing the niqab because I wasn't even thinking about it. I wore the jilbab and that was enough of a veil for me. Sarkozy and Guéant helped me decide what I thought about the full veil. Thanks to them, I feel free to exercise my faith, to wear my veil that I love with all my heart. And I'm not the only one, because there are sisters who have perhaps stopped wearing it but there are others like me who decided to wear it. Now this veil represents my freedom. Thanks, Sarkozy!

Her Business

I decided to start my business, to sell perfume, jewelry, and lingerie door-to-door. I'm supposed to get my business cards. I made my flyers. I started to order things. I'll have to travel regularly to pick up merchandise. The idea is to sell seductive things. I asked around for advice from religious scholars. It's for women's husbands or just for between women. I'm also going to sell lingerie but I don't think they'll go out in it, or wear the panties out. Islam is very simple: we have outfits for going out—the full veil. We hide our nudity. At home we do what we want, we wear what we want when no one can see except for our husbands. There are no restrictions there.

I want to sell women nice things they can wear to please their husbands, especially those women who can't go out anymore or go shopping. They're too afraid of getting assaulted or fined and they'd rather stay home. So I decided to bring the merchandise to them.

Often you hear about Muslims who say that the full veil wasn't part of religion. What I want to say to them is: what Islam do you practice? I practice the prophet Muhammad's Islam, not French Islam. I'm the one who was taken to court twice, besides I have a summons for December 21 but as usual I won't go. Do they really think their fines are going to work to make us stop wearing the veil? Especially since it's that law that led me to wear it, it gave me the clear proof that it was an obligation, it's not like I'm going to take it off overnight. They can forbid us to go out but we're not going to obey. Because we only obey Allah. If Allah tells me to be covered, I'm covered. If Allah tells me to pray, I do it. If democracy forbids me to go out, well I'd rather throw it away.

I use the texts of the laws and human rights to show their hypocrisy. But I don't refer to them myself. They don't even follow their own laws and they want us to follow them! They say that we're oppressed, imprisoned by our husbands, but who's stopping us from going out now? Our husbands? No. Who's harassing us now? Is it our husbands who're beating us? No, it's people in the street, and they insult us in front of our children. They don't care at all, they even put children in custody with their mothers, two-month-old and nine-month-old babies were locked up in a cell with their mother because she was wearing the niqab. To see a woman being modest is shocking but seeing a half-naked woman on the side of a bus stop isn't. It's all backwards!

The community is split in half. There are those who act like victims and those who won't take it passively. I chose to be a full-fledged Muslim myself, and not the kind of Muslim you can change, shape. Because my body belongs to me, it doesn't belong to the state. You massacre us all over the world. But still Islam grows, Islam is there whether you like it or not. Because our faith is so much stronger than yours. Do whatever you want to us, it won't change a thing.

Above all I'm talking to Islamophobes, to fascists, to neo-Nazis, and finally to the government.

They call us prostitutes. And yet we're mothers, human beings. It's easy to attack women, with this law the French state is attacking women. But if you're men, go after men. Attack them, insult them, you won't do it. I'm at a point where I'm like, zero tolerance. I don't forgive, I'll attack. If I'm attacked I attack.

Her Plan for Her *Hegira*

If you want to learn, don't go to the mosque. Since at the mosque they don't tell you that the hegira *is a requirement or that voting is* chirk. Lots of Muslims vote for someone who'll use human laws against us, to kill our brothers and sisters. But they don't know it. You have to buy books from trustworthy authors.

I'm 100% sure they're ready to massacre us. History repeats itself, the same thing's going to happen to us that happened to the Jews. Muslims have replaced Jews in the media. Before the threat was the Jews and now it's the Muslims. There were lots of things done to Jews that today are being done to Muslims.

So I decided to do the hegira, *to emigrate, because it's an obligation.*

On Race

Once a man who was fairly old came up and said to me, "You know that's not allowed in France." I told him, "Yes, but what's it to you?" But starting from the moment when he saw that I was Black, he drew back and left. People can't see that I'm Black from a distance. As soon as they get close, it feels like they want to say something but stop short. It's kind of amazing. Like, are you afraid because Black people do voodoo and magic, I don't know, or is it that you're still afraid of Black people?

Yes, there's racism against Blacks, but I think that racism is a lot stronger and more violent against Arabs. It shows that all the laws and constitutions don't do anything because we're subject to racism on a daily basis.

We talk about a country of laicity, freedom, equality, but there's no freedom or equality for Muslims. It's been a year that I've worn the niqab and there's been lots of hypocrisy. Éric Raoult, one of the law's proponents, was charged with domestic violence.

Excited from the beginning, Saliha often becomes very passionate about the niqab. She is radicalized in three months and succumbs to the desire for revenge for the humiliations she suffers; she refuses to compromise with the surrounding society. Her rhetoric is apocalyptic: she believes the end of the world is approaching and she wears surgical masks to protect herself from the pandemics that will destroy the world. She joins Forsane Alizza.

In 2012, she decides to leave for Tataouine after a religious marriage via the Internet with an Antillean Salafi man who has converted to Islam; she agrees to be his second wife. Her goal is to go to Syria. At the end of 2014, Alexia* updates me about her:

> *People say on social media that Saliha denounced the jihadists. But it's also possible that she's disillusioned by this form of Islam. She could have met the same kind of people in Tunisia as in Syria and Iraq and denounced them in favor of the good. I don't know what she experienced.*
>
> *I'm closer to Saliha in the way she understands Islam. I can't root for people who do bad things like kill innocent people. If she left, it was because of the pressure against the niqab. If she changed sides, it's because she understood. She took the side of the Talafi against those in favor of jihad, people who live for that alone.*

ÉMILIE KÖNIG

Convert to Islam

Figure 19. Émilie in her kitchen, May 2012.

Émilie was born in 1984 and she is twenty-seven years old when we meet for the first time. Her name was given to me by Abou Islam. Islam is a Forsane Alizza member I meet on April 20, 2012, during the rally for Mohamed Achamlane held in front of the Palais de Justice in Paris. Achamlane had been incarcerated for twenty days. On the day of the rally, Émilie, who has chosen to go by the name Samra, is stopped by the police as soon as she arrives at the Cité metro stop. I just miss her. I meet her three days later at the same place, for another Forsane rally. A "brother" buys us drinks at a café in front of the Palais. She puts on a surgical mask before entering the court. I do a quick interview with her on camera.

Émilie wants to attend the hearing for Mohamad Achamlane, arrested at home on March 30, one month after the group disbanded. But the hearing is closed, and we are asked to leave the room. She frames her surgical mask as a "small compromise."

Profile

After April 22, we have multiple exchanges in her apartment in Boulogne and over the phone. On camera, I ask her about her trajectory:

I left school at age fifteen and a half with an exception. I was a student athlete, an acrobatic gymnast at a fairly high level and my coach was encouraging and said I could go far. But I had trouble with my knee and I had to stop. Then I did training in men's and women's retail clothing and in makeup.

I had been around Muslims since childhood. I converted to Islam at seventeen and started wearing the hijab five years ago, during my second pregnancy [at age twenty-two], first in the Kabyle style and then I closed it and wore gloves, skirts, and long dresses. I've been wearing the niqab for two and a half years. A sheikh is the one who convinced me.

I married a man who had been in prison for domestic violence and then for drug trafficking. It was a shotgun marriage because I was pregnant with my second child. He was Algerian and non-practicing, he did drugs. I belonged to him, like I was his thing. When I got married, he had already been in prison. He was someone who really destroyed me, he broke my nose several times. I still have a problem with my nasal septum and I have to take medication when I have a cold. I put myself back together thanks to my sisters and to Islam.

When he got out of prison, I was still living in Lorient. I found him sitting on my bed beside me. My sons had opened the door to him. Then he locked them in their room. He yelled at me and slapped me, wanted me to get undressed, I screamed. It was to get away from him that I came to Paris last May [2011]. I found this apartment in Boulogne through work. I was an insurance broker in a call center. I only had 712 euros to live on. My husband doesn't come near me anymore because I'm not alone anymore. The brothers can come defend me so he's wary of me. I wanted to go to court to have full custody of my children but they wouldn't let me in. A Turkish man forbade me to enter even though I raised my niqab with a big smile. I made a video that I put on the Internet. That incident really hurt me.

Her two sons are only a year apart; the first is seven years old, in first grade, and the younger is six, in his second year of preschool. She confides in me that the older, unlike his brother, is not the son of the Kabyle father but a Yugoslavian, which they do not know, believing themselves to be full brothers. She speaks of this openly even though they are playing right in front of us. She continues, unabashedly, to describe her guilt at having continued to work as a bartender in a nightclub in Lorient even though she was already Muslim, as well as her relationships with men. Her children suffer from a lack of psychological stability. She is hard on them, yelling constantly.

Émilie insists that her father is Jewish and that he was born in France to Polish-Jewish parents. The first time she comes to pick me up at the Boulogne subway station, we pass by a Kosher restaurant on a Friday afternoon. She explains to me that it is soon the Sabbath and that she is familiar with the Jewish religion because of her father's roots. She claims even to have attempted to convert:

> *My father always referred to himself as "the son of immigrants and a French citizen." He left our family home when I was two or three years old and I found him again when I was eleven. I know that I wasn't wanted so I'm not mad at him for having left. He used to be a policeman and was very charismatic and kind. I love him very much. When I saw him again, I was pregnant with my second child and about to give birth, and he thought I had breast implants. When he saw the framed Quran verses he fell into a chair and said, it can't be true! I had told him that he was going to be a grandfather for the second time without saying that my son would be named Mohamed. I saw him take off in his car, knowing I wouldn't see him again. I was dead to him. I still cry, because I love him. My mother doesn't show it but she has suffered greatly. She still lives in Lorient and my boys spend their school vacations there. There are four of us kids, from three different fathers. My mother got married young, and her mother-in-law did her best to ruin everything.*
>
> *I also suffered from my mother's boyfriend who abused me from when I was eleven to when I was thirteen. I got through it by relying on religion. In God I found unconditional love, I wanted to be my best to please him. I was called by Islam. I have proof of it. I'm an activist for Islamic causes. I'm here to help my brothers and sisters. A young woman was assaulted next door and I was the one who went to help her. I've supported Forsane since the beginning. I'm an empath.*

Following the attacks carried out by Mohamed Merah, I question Émilie about the armed soldiers who patrol the streets of Paris. Merah's name makes her react immediately, and she claims to be proud: "I honor his memory." She has one desire when it comes to the soldiers: to steal their guns and use them. She asserts that she knows how to use them well and she mimes loading the magazine and firing a machine gun in front of her. She considers killing legitimate in the way a verbal retort is legitimate when someone is irritated. In her opinion, killing is permissible to defend oneself from assault or aggression. She insists on the legitimacy of killing.

Two weeks later, on May 13, 2012, she tells me she is engaged to a man she introduces as a jihadist:

> *My future husband is a convert, Belgian. He's thirty and used to live in England. He's a former companion of Bin Laden, who I admire greatly. I was very sad when I learned of his death last year. My fiancé is on lists*

worldwide for his relationship with Bin Laden. Look at his picture that he sent me, on my phone—his head is shaved because he's just back from the Umrah. You can see, his facial features and his nose and lips, he really does look like Bin Laden, like he was his son. He's the one who carried out the shooting in London. I am proud of being with a man wanted by the police and considered dangerous. But he's against Forsane Alizza and doesn't want me to speak out with them. In his opinion they're the reason there's no unity in the ummah.

On May 29, I return to film her at home in Boulogne. She wears a dark blue jilbab and a black niqab. Before I turn on the camera, she tells the story of her son being possessed the night before by a *"shaytan."* Her story is dramatized, told to maximize fear; she mimics her son's contortions, all resembling a scene from the movie "The Exorcist":

He was stretched out on his stomach on the bed, his knees bent. Then he flattened himself against the wall, his face twisted, his eyes staring at the television. He spit in my face, shouting "I hate you" at me. I saved him by yelling, "Shaytan! Get out of my son!" Immediately he started crying, saying he didn't believe what he had just said. Luckily I had access to the roqya *[Muslim exorcism]. I put on a CD of psalmody from the Quran—the Sourate Al-Baqura—for its protective value. He was still moving like a worm, on his stomach on the floor, wriggling. I knew my son was no longer possessed when he suddenly fell asleep in my arms and was calm again. I left the CD on all night.*

The CD is still on a loop when I arrive. In the face of my astonishment toward the possession, she tells me that her mother has photos of her children and uses them for acts of clairvoyance. She describes her as a seer who uses a pendulum over the photos, and she believes that these acts, which she doesn't quite condemn, could be at the origin of the possession. Another cause could be her fiancé, with whom she has just broken up.

Although she was singing his praises during my previous visit to her home two weeks before, now she detests him. They were to have been married this month. But she has just learned that he had planned to marry an eighteen-year-old girl the next Ramadan. She feels taken advantage of. She is particularly angry that he posted a nude picture of her, which he had asked her to send him, on Facebook. Several times she expresses her disillusionment. She puts down everything that had made him heroic in her eyes before, and now thinks of him as pathetic. She no longer has any matrimonial plans.

Four years later, in January 2016, I ask Alexia,* a former active member of Forsane Alizza, about these events, of which Émilie has kept her apprised:

When her Belgian fiancé asked her to send nude pictures, she did it. Samra took photos of herself standing up in her bathtub. She was scared of losing him. She imagined that by sending him her picture, she'd have him eating out of her hand. She is so submissive to men, but dominating towards women. The guy saw a woman who was pro-jihad, he lied to her with Bin Laden, made it seem like they were friends. Samra had idealized Bin Laden, she made him a hero. Today it seems like there are only his clones. To be "the" Muslim man, you have to look like Bin Laden. When he put that picture up on Facebook, she was panicked. She had to go to Facebook to get it taken down. I see her actions as a lapse, motivated by her tendency to be emotionally dependent. Deep down Samra has a disturbed personality, even after converting to Islam. She married an honest man but it lasted only a few days. He was too wholesome for someone who spent such a long time in an unwholesome milieu. I'm like Samra, we always get together with the same kind of rough guy—like her, I go for tattooed guys.

Émilie told me that she met a Saudi Arabian on a dating site who was studying medicine in Germany. But she turns against him when he asks that she remove the niqab while he is finishing his studies:

I refused the brother's hand. I don't have to take off my niqab. I have disavowed the dounya *[material world], it is out of the question that I would go back to my old positions which are now sins for me.*

She heaps praise on Abu Hamza, or Mohamed Achamlane, the leader of Forsane Alizza, who was arrested two months earlier. She does not hide her fascination for two other radical groups, Sharia4Belgium and Sharia4UK. Alexia* reminisces about Émilie:

I knew Samra during the Forsane Alizza days. The first time I had any interaction with her, it was because she wanted to join the group. Her request was refused because Abu Hamza wasn't taking anyone else. But she also had her accounts frozen, like the others, but on a list by herself. I thought from the beginning that she was an infiltrator because she put herself first so much—I thought it was bizarre. She was always exaggerating. She wanted to be a public persona.

We were never on the same wavelength. She was a "warrior," whereas I'm a pacifist. Still, Samra was a really nice girl, fun, emphatic, openhearted. She wanted to do good in the world around her.

Samra didn't become ghulat. *She never went as far as I did. She hung out with jihadists. That was why she supported Mohammed Merah,[7] but would have agreed to go to the town hall to get married, complete with* livret de famille *(official family record book)*. *I was the exact opposite: I was against Merah and against the administration. I got to know other* ghulat *with my ex-husband after I spent time with Forsane Alizza. The* ghulat *aren't jihadists, since they pronounce* takfir *against them. Their websites are still active, they haven't been banned since they weren't calling for jihad.*

Émilie confides in me about the state of her health; she has recovered in the past from ovarian cancer. Today she suffers from abdominal attacks. She thinks they are caused by polyps that signal cancer or Crohn's disease, but she does not seek treatment. Instead, she prefers to wait to marry, become pregnant, and give birth before being treated. She holds her body as an instrument for making children—less as an object of pleasure or desire (as Alexia* does) than an object of reproduction.

On June 6, 2012, she makes a different kind of declaration:

I want to become a writer, I have a history I need to tell. I want to be a reporter, to post pictures as the bombs fall. It's a kind of therapy. I'm in love with words and could do it all at home, on the Internet: I could get my DEAU [a diploma necessary to study at the university level] and enroll in a psychology undergraduate degree. I'm interested in all aspects of psychology and philosophy.

Émilie leaves for Syria several months later, leaving her children's education to her mother. Alexia* has remained in touch with her via Facebook and updates me regularly, before losing contact in 2014:

She crossed the Syrian border totally uncovered, without even her hijab. That was her trick for going incognito. When she said on camera for you that she wanted to go to Yemen, it was to protect herself. She wasn't going to confess that she was getting ready to go to Syria. If you had published, she would have immediately been under surveillance. She had been planning to go fight for a long time.

Samra was a wounded soul. She was saying: "For me, it's more important to go do hegira *than to take care of my kids." She was very controversial there. She shared too much of her life in public. She recruited people from Syria; she thought she was doing good for Muslims. Samra couldn't stay here anymore with her niqab: now there's the Islamic State and nothing left for her to do in France. We both wore the niqab to live in peace. But we differed greatly in our understanding of Islam.*

In Syria, Émilie gets together with Axel Baeza (Abou Mohamed), a French convert. She sends pictures of herself. They have a son first, and then twins. He is killed in combat, and then Émilie is arrested in Syria in December 2017 by Kurdish YPG forces and detained in a Syrian camp. She appears bareheaded on January 8, 2018, in a YPG press propaganda video. On July 5, 2022, she was among sixteen mothers repatriated to France. As soon as she arrived in France, she was indicted for association with terrorist criminals. She is now in custody.

Figure 20. From the documentary *Émilie König vs Ummu Tawwab* (2016). The Al-Qaeda flag covers her television during my first visit in April 2012, but not during my subsequent visits.

Figure 21. Video posted on YouTube, addressed to her two sons on June 1, 2013, showing her firing a machine gun. She promises to meet them in Paradise, signaling her desire not to return.

NAÏMA S.

Parents of Algerian Origin

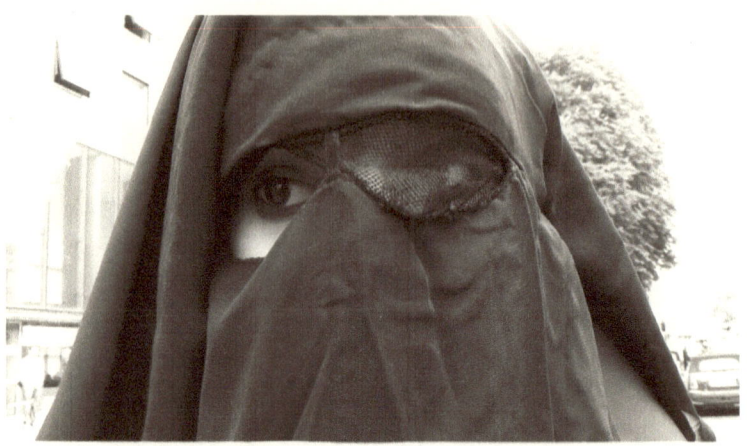

Figure 22. Naïma when I meet her for the first time on October 6, 2011, exiting the maternity ward after having been separated from her daughter for six days.

Naïma is a victim on multiple levels. Raped by her father and her brother, committed to a psychiatric hospital by her mother, raped again by a man who took her home, and blamed by her husband as responsible for these sexual assaults, she loses custody in January 2019 of her youngest daughter, who is born in 2018 and placed into foster care.

Naïma compensates for her failures by a sympathy for the Islamic State which she expresses freely. She is arrested on January 6, 2020, at the Gare d'Austerlitz train station in Paris while in possession of a knife and a Quran. Whether she is in a psychiatric hospital or in prison, it is impossible to find her today.

Our First Meeting

On October 5, 2011, I am contacted by Lila,* the president of "Amazons for Freedom." She tells me about a woman who gave birth to her first child via a C-section in a hospital in Aubervilliers. This woman put her niqab back on after giving birth, which led to trouble with the medical staff who had her record of depression on file. According to Lila,* the medical team had subjected the woman to psychological pressure, taking her daughter away for six days under the pretext of her medical history, all the way to the point of threatening to keep her, judging the woman incapable of taking care of her.

The next day I show up at the hospital and meet Naïma at the exit. She is twenty-nine years old and wears a niqab with a black gauze veil covering only one eye. Her eyes are heavily made up with kohl, giving them a smoky look. She agrees to go on camera. But when I ask her to adjust her veil over both eyes, she responds that she wanted the asymmetrical effect, which seems to me almost Goth in style. Her sister and her husband, with his beard and his *quamis*, are with her and wait for her in the car. Naïma speaks to the camera as if she is appearing on television before an imaginary public that she wants to shock with the story of what she has just undergone. She recounts having to convince the medical personnel to keep her daughter in her room: "They try to make me out as crazy because I'm under psychiatric supervision, even crazier than I am."

Profile

Naïma was born in the north of France in 1982, the fifth child out of seven siblings (five girls and two boys). She has a younger brother and a younger sister. Her father came to France from Algeria and was a trucker. She describes her mother as a Kabyle, born in France. Her parents divorced in 1998, when Naïma was thirteen. Naïma has no religious education except for what she learned of Catholicism while in private school:

> *I didn't have a Muslim upbringing. I went to a Catholic school. My mother had decided that that was a better education. I had required catechism classes.*
>
> *At school I didn't know that I was Muslim—I didn't even know what a hijab was. For me then, modesty meant jeans and sneakers. I only knew that I was Arab, which people reminded me about pretty often, so I didn't forget. You start feeling the effects of racism in elementary school. The others didn't want to play with me. From 1998 to 2005 in Nord-Pas-de-Calais, we lived in public housing where the majority of people were "originally" French; it was a mining district where the people were the most racist. We had neighbors who even insulted the people who came to visit us. There were physical fights and I got a cracked rib. My father got punched leaving the house but of course there was no media attention. It was a real jihad. No one in my family wore the veil. A gap has arisen between me and the* kuffar. *Finally we went to live in La Creuse.*[8]

Naïma is the only one of her siblings to be attracted to religion:

When I was thirteen and my parents separated, I failed out of school. I was a really good student until middle school but by the time I got to high school I was totally behind. My friends served as a springboard towards something new: Islam. When I was fourteen I observed Ramadan all by myself. But I wasn't veiled, I was still trying to get attention.

When I was around nineteen, I wanted to get married. I was so ignorant that I thought it was physical appearance that men wanted. It was so stupid. You can't throw yourself into the fray like that in front of people, especially men, even if it's to find a husband. But that's how I was thinking. I dyed my hair, I wore makeup. I really regret that time of my life. It was shaytan *who told me: Go get married, look, if you wear your make up like this and you do your hair like that you'll find a husband. When you're young, even fifteen, you want to see if you look good, it's the middle of your psychological development. I was really influenced by women's magazines, like those my mother read. My mother named me Nahema when I was born, which was the name of a Guerlain perfume that came out in 1980. She was fascinated by the world of fashion and that influenced me. I thought I was a model and I wanted attention. I would watch a show on [the TV channel] M6: "The Shopping Queens."*

But when I was twenty-two, I met a real jerk, a shaytan. *He was a man from the North African community. I agreed to get in his car because I was in trouble but he wanted to get something out of it. He wanted to go have a drink but I didn't feel like it. One night he called me around 10 P.M. and gave me his usual spiel. I wasn't attracted to him, he was ugly. My mother took the phone and thought he was nice. I don't understand what happened with my mother because she was always the first to tell me not to go out. It was sorcery. She trusted him because he was North African, like us. He came to get me in his car. I realized he was getting on the highway and he said we were going to Lille. Actually he took me to his house in Dunkerque. It was midnight. He was threatening. He was making tea in his kitchen like one of those psychopaths in American films, with the victim waiting. He told me, "You're scared that I'm doing sorcery?" I wasn't afraid, even though with sorcery you can do anything to people. I escaped into the street. He caught up with me by car and he was mad. I ran but he got even madder. I felt threatened, I was overwhelmed. I got into the car and in the car he started touching me and raped me. I was crying. After that he took me home.*

Before, in my childhood, I was the victim of rape by my father, as were my little brother and little sister, and then the victim of rape by my older brother. My mother knew but she had been beaten herself by my father.

Our family has problems. For my whole childhood I thought I was a prostitute.

After what happened to me in Dunkerque I decided to wear the hijab. But it wasn't possible in the infidel milieu then. There was no Muslim bookstore. I really struggled to start wearing the hijab, especially since I had no money. I realized that Islam was the opposite of seduction, that Muslim women know they shouldn't try to attract men's gazes. Right after that I started praying—that was in March 2004. There was no one to explain things to me. I bought a book to learn how to pray. When I was twenty-five, I started wearing the black veil.

Her religious journey leads to no professional or personal success. On the contrary: in 2009, when she is twenty-seven and wearing the jilbab, she and her mother are evicted. Even with a modest rent, her mother cannot pay the expenses. This eviction is very difficult for Naïma, who speaks about it often:

One morning the police arrived with a bailiff. They didn't even bother to knock on the door, they took out the lock. My little sister was shocked, too. I got very depressed. I spent time in the hospital at my and my mother's request. Spiritually I was very fragile. To live in precarity all the time is really hard.

Naïma's mother pays the rent alone. Naïma could have earned a living but has never had a profession; nor have her little brother and sister, who are in their twenties. All three depend on their mother in difficult social circumstances.

After leaving the psychiatric hospital, Naïma continues her matrimonial quest:

I joined a dating site, muslima.com. I got into contact with a man who asked if I was one of the salafiyya. *At the time I didn't know what that meant. I must have seemed stupid to him, I told him that I wanted to learn but he didn't contact me again. After that I started doing research on the Internet. I typed the word* salafiyya *into Google and I found Salafist doctrine. I said to myself: I want to learn, I immersed myself in it. After that I required all my contacts on muslima.com to belong to the group that imitates the Prophet. That's how I met my husband. The first thing I asked was if he was* minhaj *[the Salafi way]. He said yes,* inchallah.

She has a religious marriage at age twenty-eight. Her husband is an undocumented Tunisian who comes from Tataouine. He has been in France for six years. The couple are civilly unioned, thinking that they will be able to attain his residence permit quickly:

He arrived in France when he was twenty-five. When I met him, I discovered a whole new universe. His parents were practicing Muslims but not Salafi. They were old country people. I think he became Salafi when he arrived in France, it must have disgusted him to see all the women half-naked and that was the moment he was radicalized. He said anyway it was when he got to France that he started growing his beard. For our religious marriage, I had no witnesses, no mahram. *He asked a brother he knew to serve as my tutor. My family rejected my marriage because he was Salafi and had a beard. They wanted me to get it annulled.*

After my marriage, I told my husband about the sexual abuse I had suffered, although I should have told him before. At first he seemed understanding. But when we slept together and there was no blood, he understood. He couldn't go through with it. He changed completely. He always brings up the thing that happened in Dunkerque and tells me, "You're just a piece of shit." That already cost me weeks of therapy. He was already causing me problems before marriage. I don't understand why I married him.

Her older sister is a municipal employee. She is not religious, wears makeup, and "doesn't pray yet." I met her with Naïma at the exit of the maternity ward. She calls me to tell me the story of Naïma and her husband:

They met on a Muslim dating site. At the time, she was living in La Creuse with our mother. It went over very badly: what, you're going to Paris to get married even though you've never spent any time together and he's undocumented! She didn't listen to us and left for Aubervilliers to live with him. But one day she sends me a text to come get her. So we picked her up. But they kept in touch. Naïma went away with him again. She was twenty-eight and didn't know anything about men up to that point. There were disagreements from the beginning, when he wanted to marry a second wife. It's been really hard for our family.

The Niqab

When I met him, my husband talked about the niqab but he didn't insist on it. I was the one who one day just asked him to go buy me one. It was a decision I made on my own, three or four months after we got married. I started wearing the niqab when Sarkozy was president, so right in the middle of the controversy around the law banning face coverings. At first I was scared and I talked about it with my husband. He said, "It doesn't matter, we must follow Allah and his prophet." So one day he bought me one, he brought it home and from that day on I went out with my face covered. I discovered it was a blessing; wearing it convinced me. I feel protected, it's relaxing, but the main reason for it is religion. The niqab isn't a closing off from others. We live in an infidel country that prevents women from living.

Naïma is a vulnerable woman with a record of dependency, taking both antipsychotics and antidepressants. She rushes headlong into religion. Her husband plays the role of a mentor, creating a relationship of dominance over his wife/disciple. She does experience moments of lucidity during which she refuses the proposed agreement and returns to her family. But she quickly falls back into her husband's grasp. Even if she complains about him to her friends and family, she never blames him and she shrinks before him, making the situation hard to witness for her loved ones, who are unsure how to help. Her permanent ambivalence ultimately discourages them. We might almost call this a sort of "psychiatric niqab," explaining her need to hide her face, like a straitjacket.

In April 2017, after another stay in the psychiatric hospital for depression, she tells me that her first daughter, born in 2011, lives in Tataouine with her paternal grandparents to keep her out of foster care. She keeps her second child, a four-year-old boy, with her. On camera, she takes up the thread of her story, recounting an episode that particularly marked her, and that her husband uses to make her feel guilty:

When I was younger, I tried to go into training to be a police officer. I had good grades but I wasn't hired because I couldn't provide the certified medical certificate. I wanted to become a police officer because all my life it's bothered me to see injustice, to see pedophiles and drug dealers going free. For me it wasn't about subjugating Arabs in the street, obviously not. I wanted to bring justice. In the end I failed, it was mektoub, *fate. Allah chose another path for me. A few years after that I started wearing the jilbab and then the niqab,* alhamdullilah.

I'm sorry I attempted the training when I see now that the bad guys aren't who we think they are. You think you're doing good but like Allah says in the Quran: those who think they're doing good although they believe neither in Allah nor in judgment day are the ones who are lost. Yes, I'm sorry, I feel like I betrayed Muslims. My husband reproaches me for it constantly.

She gives an account of her last police arrest:

You have to plan to sneak out so you don't run into an Islamophobe or the police. It's awful. I remember it well, September 28, 2016. I meet a

> *police officer who wants to fine me for covering my face. I say to myself, well ok, I'll take off my niqab so he can check my identity and that'll be the end of it. Underneath my niqab I had a surgical mask. He didn't like that either. He told me, "No, take off your mask." I told him I had health problems. He wouldn't listen. Other officers arrived as reinforcements and said, "You don't want to take it off, we'll take you away." I said, "No, wait, I'll show you my face but then I'll put it back on." They said, "Too late, we're taking you to the station."*
>
> *They took me off with my son. One of the cops was really worked up, he said, "If you want to dress like that, go to Saudi Arabia." I told him, "You're all happy to go to our countries, to the beach in Tunisia or Morocco or Dubai." He says to me, "Yes but when we're there we obey the rules." Another giant lie. I was in Tunisia a few times and the French women went around in short shorts in Tataouine. We don't stop them from dressing how they want.*
>
> *They kept us in the cell for an hour. The woman cop searched me again. The other cop said to me: "What do you think you're doing? You are going to take off that veil you're wearing, you're not keeping that veil on your head." I said, "Listen, there's no law banning covering your hair. I'm not taking it off." I called him perverse and sadistic and that stopped him. After that he left the cell.*
>
> *My son started getting stressed. He was fidgeting on the bench, overwhelmed. My son is intelligent. He's sharp for his age, he understood that his mom got stopped and taken in because of what I was wearing. I told him, "That's what* kuffar *do, see what they do to Muslims." The day after the incident he wet his bed even though he hasn't done that since he was two. He turned four in February. For a few months he was repeating, "The cops are mean."*

Off camera, she has no trouble expressing her hatred for the police and her satisfaction at seeing the acts of terrorism that target law enforcement. She sees herself as a victim of injustice and is deeply resentful:

> *It's crazy to be monitored like this! To be policed so much, it's incredible. We're in the suburbs, in Seine-Saint-Denis [the northern suburb of Paris], there are so many people from other places but paradoxically we can't live here anymore. They banned me from entering my son's school. The principal told me, "Leave your child with another mother and she'll drop him off at school." I said, "That's out of the question, I will take my son to his classroom." It's too much!*

Her speech becomes increasingly aggressive and her references to the state more explicit:

> We've lost all prospects in Syria since the Islamic State's lost ground. Jihad is a noble cause. But it's not easy, it's not for everyone to go blow themselves up. That requires a lot of courage. You have to have rock-solid faith. Among the jihadists there are quite a few converts, people who live in stable places and have family lives, balanced lives. At a certain moment when you see that there's injustice, you have to react. The jihadists fight with what they have. But look at the number of missiles the coalition launches every day.
>
> This worldly life is a prison for believers and a paradise for infidels. When you see the young kids going to fight in Syria on the news, it's because they understand that the true meaning of life isn't in this dounya. They're going to make their entrance into paradise ready, for themselves and their loved ones. Islam isn't a religion of hatred but you can't lie to yourself when you see what the American GIs did during the Iraq war, they raped Muslim women. That's why a certain resistance branch was created. We had Al-Qaeda, now it's the Islamic State. We can no longer make the bad guys like the good guys and the good guys look like horrible cutthroats, no, it's more complicated than that.
>
> The law against the niqab that was passed in 2010 sparked a feeling of injustice. The most docile sheep follow their government's path. As soon as they see me in the street they scream, they insult me and call after me saying that it's banned. It doesn't shock me that people take revenge for women's honor, for Muslim women's dignity.
>
> When they target Muslim women, they also target Muslim men. By attacking women they want to destroy Islam, they're keeping Muslims from living. When I hear them say that it's the husband who makes his wife wear the niqab, that's a serious problem. It's well known that in France it's the women who want to wear the niqab. They want to destroy Muslim men by saying they're forcing their wives. When my daughter was born and we went to the pediatrician, the doctor thought I was some poor woman subjugated by her husband. It hurts Muslim men when the infidel state accuses them of oppressing their wives. They want to strip us, undress us. It's humiliating.

Her hatred of the *kuffar* grows stronger on each one of my visits. I try to understand the origin of this repudiation more deeply, asking her about the kind of prejudice to which she was subject. She traces it back to the day she was wearing the veil and her former friends turned their backs on her. After an initial bafflement, she ultimately realized the true character of the *kuffar* who want to eliminate Muslims, according to her, and would do anything to make them disappear, as proved by the acts of violence committed against Muslims, which she enjoys enumerating. She understands current attacks in Europe as rightful vengeance against humiliation:

> I can't stand the kuffar—*they do harm to Muslims and I'm against the infidel governments and those who follow them. They're part of the party of Shaytan.*

Naïma's remarks concerning her hatred of "infidels" cannot be generalized; very few niqab wearers express this type of reaction.

On September 21, 2017, I accompany her to family court in Bobigny, at which Naïma and her husband risk losing custody of their son. Her husband surprises me in his cheerful appearance; he appears easygoing by contrast to Naïma, with her closed and anxious face. When I ask her if her husband is going to shake the judge's hand, she says she has talked about it with him, knowing that both of them will be tried and tested for their "radicalism." Naïma is categorical: "My husband is not allowed to shake hands with the judge." I suggest that such resistance might have consequences that go beyond a simple gesture. But Naïma shuts down, saying, "They have absolutely no modesty!" Her husband, on the other hand, says he is willing to shake the judge's hand in the interest of their son. He even advises his wife to do the same with a man if necessary. But Naïma sticks to her principles and refuses any compromise, even temporarily.

Naïma returns to the violence she has suffered, sketching out a typology:

> *The law has unleashed the infidels' hatred, whereas before people just ignored women wearing the niqab. The women who attack me are between fifty and sixty years old or even older. They're mostly overweight and unattractive. They're physically unkempt, not well-groomed. They're ugly and mean. But then others are extremely elegant and made up, with their hair styled. They're either sloppy or totally elegant. The men are also between fifty and sixty but some are younger. That's more rare.*
>
> *These Western women assault me like I've physically bumped into them, like I'm oppressing them. They yell hysterically. An old Antillean woman attacked me verbally on a bus. A young woman wanted to intervene and almost got hit with her cane. That woman was in her thirties and wearing a very low-cut shirt. Given her clothing, I was surprised that she defended me. I've never had problems with women*

who are comfortable with their bodies. May Allah guide them, for they have so much value, and it's a shame that they dress like that. But with women who are obese, it's a whole different story. I think it's the way they were raised. I feel like those women never wore mini-skirts even in their twenties or thirties. Women like that have complexes about their bodies and they've always been closed-minded.

I'm holding firm to the niqab, I'm not going to lie low just because of the kuffar. *Allah keeps me going. The most disgusting thing is that the people who are most aggressive are Arabs, like the woman in the doctor's waiting room who started shouting at me like she'd seen a* shaytan *even though it was the exact opposite. She must have been about sixty-five. Certain Arabs are even more shocked than native French people and they spit on us. They disgust me, they're forgetting that they have a religion and forgetting where they come from. It's especially the old ladies and the non-practicing Muslim women with their heads uncovered. They only want to show how civilized they are, more French than the French. A few times waiting for a doctor I've seen one of those women get all keyed up when she sees me go after another woman trying to take sides against me. The veiled woman isn't going to say a thing, she's going to agree and bow her head probably to avoid conflict and not to contradict the old hag who's getting worked up all alone, but it's a very bad thing because then she is giving in to the infidels. I was the same way when I was younger, I tended to erase myself when the* kuffar *argued against me. There's less and less solidarity between Muslim women. I am shocked by the women who wear the hijab but come out against the niqab: they're going outside of Islam.*

In October 2017, she brings up her relationship with her husband again, as it collapses:

My husband is using religion to usurp power, like for example having four wives. We've been together for seven years and I've just learned he's religiously married to three other women. He might have even been already married when we first met. We had a civil union because he wanted to get his papers. But a sister in the Courcouronnes mosque told me that a civil union, like a city hall marriage, is a pact with the infidels. The most extreme never do that. But now I think that that might have protected me, more than a civil union. It's strange to say that. A town hall marriage can protect you, it's in writing, unlike a religious marriage. He manipulated me to get his papers. He was so nice when we got married and he changed after he had what he wanted. I have a

> *girlfriend in the same situation; she got married to a guy who just wanted his residence permit. After he got it he started beating her and she even lost a baby because of it. Don't you believe that my husband is nice! We're religiously divorced, is what he told everyone even though he hasn't yet said the* talaq *[divorce, the man's initiative].*

Naïma is pregnant for the third time. She very calmly accuses her husband of having abused and raped her, although her story has elements of the incredible:

> *It might seem unbelievable but I'm not crazy. I know I was raped in my sleep, because we had no sexual relations at the time and I got pregnant. I never cheated on him. He drugged me with GHB and raped me. I remember waking up and seeing my husband and a tall Black man leaving my room. I was scared so I went to double check. Another time the tall Black man was stretched out next to me in my bed. When I asked my husband about it he slapped me. He was prostituting me in my sleep. He did it to punish me, not for the money. Once I was at the window cleaning. I saw the tall Black man and recognized him right away. He's a friend of my brothers-in-law who live next door.*
>
> *He's making me pay for my sin of having accepted an unknown man's help and getting into his car. He thinks of me as a prostitute, he calls our child the son of a whore. He's using Sharia law and he's sure Allah's on his side.*

When I question her about the "tall Black man" she responds that he was "the *shaytan*." Frequently she uses the expression, "it was like being in an American movie." I begin to wonder if she has been influenced by Roman Polanski's film *Rosemary's Baby*: like the film's heroine, she imagines she is pregnant by the devil. Another Polanski film, *Repulsion* (1963), also seems to match her personality. Some of her reactions to men that I witnessed, in the subway or at the exit of a crowded mosque on a Friday, are similar to Catherine Deneuve's in that movie, as is her story:

> *Sometimes I'm possessed. I hear voices that order me to leave Islam behind because I've sinned too much. Then I'm drowning in another world, where the* shaytan *speaks in my friends and family's voices. That kind of experience ends in the psych ward. I had problems before when I was twenty-three and twenty-four. You have to remember that the* illuminati *[term for a group of conspirators who secretly control the world] are Satanists who adore* shaytan. *This is 2017 and it still exists.*

Two weeks before her due date, she decides to leave her husband. She goes to the hospital by bus, hoping to be admitted. But there, she is taken to the psychiatrist who wants to commit her, rebuking her for not having taken her medication. Then he lets her leave:

> *After I escaped from the psychiatrist yesterday, I got stopped by the cops in front of the station, they bullied me, then a big Black man arrived and tore off my sunglasses, and then they fined me after pressuring me for an hour. It was pure police violence. When they saw the catheter attached to my hand, they took me back to the hospital. Then the hospital called my husband to come get me even though I was trying to escape him. In the hospital I filed a complaint against my husband, I told them I was the victim of domestic abuse and they went and told him. They say they want to liberate women from their husbands but they took me right back to him.*

I meet her again on March 11, 2019, in a shelter for female victims of domestic violence in Saint-Denis. She has made an agreement: to remove her niqab in exchange for free lodging. She tells me that her youngest daughter has been in foster care since January 29:

> *I left with my daughter to go to Le Havre without telling anyone and I was trying to find an apartment. Finally I ended up in a shelter because I didn't have anywhere to go. The shelter directors disliked me right away, they pigeonholed me. They started asking questions about Islam. My daughter got put into foster care. I only have the right to see her once a week, the family court decided. It's so hard not to see your baby, she's sixteen months old. The prosecutor decided that. They accused me of being an extremist, of radicalism, always the same lies to catch Muslims. They said I was scared of the exterior world and of men and that I was overprotective of my daughter.*
>
> *Their constant theme is to fight us on all fronts, or attacking the veil, the beard, really all the little details that are so important in the life of Muslim men and women. But I think that Muslims always win, dead or alive. Our reward is in paradise, the firdaous, so I'm not worried about that.*
>
> *There are lots of sisters who wore the niqab and the sitar, who left France because they couldn't stand being attacked for their modesty and their honor. We tried a few times to leave for Syria but our families got in our way. First once I wanted to leave alone, I was always on the Mejliss el kalam site, I was a regular. An Islamic State brother, Ahmed, wanted*

to get me to go to Egypt. He was a recruiter and he contacted me first. There were a few recruiters on Mejliss, members of the Islamic State. But I told my mother about it and she was against it. So was my husband's mother when we wanted to both go. And then I'd just had my son so it didn't happen. Now I regret it, I'll regret it till I die.

The brothers and sisters who went to Syria and Iraq went for the Caliphate. It was at the peak of its fame and glory then. Now there's nothing in Syria if you go, no Islamic State. They lost in Syria. But they can't kill our ideology just by launching missiles—that just strengthens our faith and our conviction.

It wasn't the real Islamic State. The real Caliphate is going to be established permanently. The golden age will arrive even if not right away—we have to wait. It's going to happen inchallah, *my faith is firm in this, like all Muslims.*

France is oppressive for Muslims. They made a law stopping women from wearing their clothes. It's totally grotesque. My husband told me to wear the surgical mask but even in the mask people say things. They figured it out and they banned that too. I've been arrested wearing the surgical mask, it's unbelievable. At my son's school they made a scene because I was wearing it.

A week later, she suggests that I go with her to see her daughter in Villepinte. She passes me off as her cousin, since only family members have visiting rights. I witness the effusion of joy between mother and child. But the visit is short and Naïma leaves angry:

Those two social aides were constantly hassling me. They were two hyenas, they're skinny, so well-kept, totally rotten. It was like I was mentally worthless, like I might not even be able to use the restroom. They said I was giving my daughter (twenty-one months) inappropriate toys, either above or below her age. I said that I had her play cooking games. They accused me of influencing her. They think I'm wrong for not having her play dolls, those shaytan-*faced plastic prostitutes [Barbie dolls]. It's never good enough for them. But then both of them like my husband even though he's on the police watchlist and engages in* taqiyya *[dissimulation].*

We didn't have a lawyer. But I'm ready to do anything: as Allah says in the Quran, "Attack them with all the means you have at your disposition. Light or heavy, throw yourself into battle." So I'm going to get a lawyer. If I can kidnap her I'll do it. I can't last another six months without her. It's more than I have in me.

In December 2019, I again accompany her to see her daughter on their weekly visit. She tells me about having wanted to carry out a knife attack on the last Pride parade in Paris (the previous June 29) but having changed her mind at the last moment. She confides that she has pledged allegiance to the Islamic State and stopped her monthly injections of Xepilon (a drug for schizophrenia), and then she continues, with emotion:

They want to make me crack but I'm holding on. I won't give anything up, not the niqab or my daughter. For me those are the two essentials, like my two eyes. The jilbab is my left eye and my daughter is my right eye. What I want from the Islamic State is first, for us to be able to wear the niqab and the veil freely; second, for Allah's laws to be applied; and third, to get rid of the kuffar.

Over the phone, she tells me that she's found new public housing. But as soon as her invectives against the *kuffar* start up again, I ask her to no longer contact me. We are last in touch via text message on December 18. Less than two weeks later, she is arrested at the Gare d'Austerlitz train station while in possession of a knife and a Quran—the end of a long trajectory.

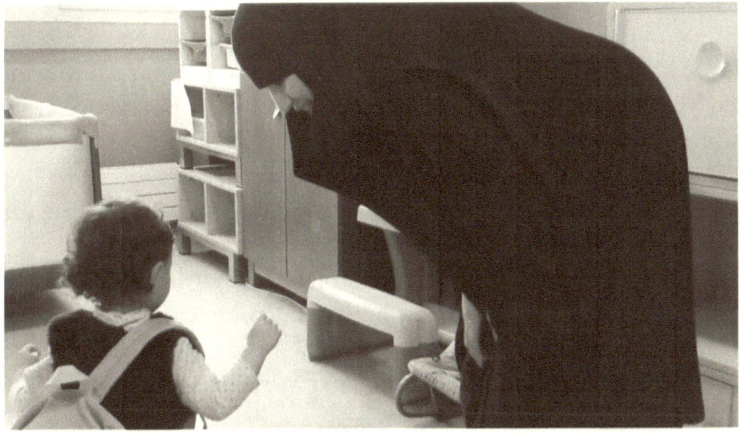

Figure 23. Naïma and her daughter during their weekly visit on March 21, 2019, two months after she was placed into foster care.

MANON

Convert to Islam

Figure 24. Manon at the Annual Meeting of French Muslims in Le Bourget, 2017.

I meet Manon for the first time on April 17, 2017, at the Annual Meeting of French Muslims in the northeastern French suburb of Le Bourget. She is wearing a black niqab and is accompanied by her husband, who is bearded and wears a qamis, as well as her fifteen-month-old son in a stroller. She is twenty-three years old at the time and started wearing the niqab three years earlier, before her marriage to a Salafi man.

I approach her and describe my film project, inviting her to speak on camera. She has difficulty deciding; her husband, too, appears shy and reserved. Both say they would like time to think about it. I agree and ask them to stay in contact. I see her several times after this, and we speak regularly by telephone.

Profile

Manon was born in 1994 in the Poitou-Charentes region. Her parents were school janitors, and she trained as a beautician. She recounts her yearning for spirituality during her atheist upbringing. She turned first to Catholicism, the only religion she knew. She asked to be baptized and made her first communion. It was in high school in Poitiers that she encountered Islam for the first time, in 2010. At the age of sixteen, she fell severely ill. Today she sees a link between her conversion and her recovery. (It should be noted that 2010 was also the year that the ban on the full veil was passed and its accompanying media hype.) She began wearing the niqab in 2014, at age nineteen. Her parents accepted her conversion to Catholicism but were more hesitant about Islam. She marries (religiously) a Tunisian man with whom she has a son and from whom she is separated; the latter is with her at Le Bourget. She tells her story concerning the niqab:

> I wore the niqab in France after coming back from Egypt, where I never had any problems. But I'd started wearing it when I was nineteen, before I met my husband. He never pushed me to wear it. It's Allah's command to protect myself and save myself for my closest relatives, and also to protect me from men, all of that. At the beginning I didn't wear it all the time, at the time I was living at my parents' home and it wouldn't even have been imaginable to wear the niqab.
>
> I met my husband through friends. But after, it was a real shock when I saw the woman he left with. He met her on a trip to Spain and she was wearing short shorts and a tank top. He thought she was beautiful and married her. He convinced me that we'd be friends and she'd help take care of our child. He left me when I was two months pregnant and he never kept those promises. My son is two years old now and he's what keeps me holding on. I don't want him to become like his father. Some men basically use Salafi as an excuse to behave badly, to cheat on women and have it be religiously legal. We think of them as gone astray.

Manon is vegetarian and buys only organic groceries. She punctuates her sentences with Hadiths that contradict her resentment: "There are many blessings in accepting polygamy," "In Paradise women will have one husband, we don't know which, while men will be surrounded by many women."

I suggest we go together to see Naïma* at her house in the Aubervilliers suburb; both women are single following their husband's infidelities. I am curious about their potential conversation. Soon, a bond forms based on similarity of lived experience. Both have a violent father, capable of unprovoked physical abuse; both suffer daily insults and want to make their *hegira*. Manon aspires to go to Egypt, a country she has loved since she was there for eight months with her husband in 2013, but she is conscious of the impasse that the country has been in since Abdel Fattah el-Sisi's coup in 2014.

Both of them share one source of trouble: polygamy. Their suffering, they reveal, is a major taboo in the Muslim community. Manon dreams of a divorce—a far cry from her pious Hadiths, glorifying the status of co-wife.

Naïma* goes further:

I have never understood women who praise polygamy. Some of them go so far as to find wives for their husband, otherwise it's a lack of faith. Mine thinks of the right to four women like it's a given. I recently learned that I had co-wives in Tunisia. I've often been very upset about the subject.

In October of 2017, Manon reports the verbal aggressions she is subject to in public:

I've heard it all, obviously from native French people but also from Arab mothers wearing the veil. One of them told me, "You make us ashamed, that's not what Islam is." Even Black people take us to task.

When I go to the countryside to see my mother who lives near Poitiers, the kids also attack me: "It's not Halloween!" Really, it's everyone. The kids don't say anything in the city but they feel free in the country. It's like people become good citizens by reminding us about order or even insulting us. With a husband people are much less daring. I've never filed a complaint and I won't, ever, because they'd just refuse it right away. I was stopped by the police for wearing the sitar at the market. People in the street are awful, they think of themselves as the police. It's like in the age of the Gestapo, when people denounced their neighbors. They tell us, "We're in France."

She returns to her love affair:

Before I wasn't living in reality. I wore the sitar, I didn't even go out for errands. My husband did them. I only went to the doctor and to the pharmacy in the neighborhood. I was totally naïve, totally lost in religion. At the time things were good with my husband, I was blindly in love, totally enraptured.

That lasted three years and it was amazing. We went to Egypt to learn Arabic and came back to France. My husband started his business and I began to see his faults. Then there was his second marriage and that changed everything. Today it's every person for themselves and I manage by myself. I wish that our happiness hadn't ended like that.

Manon stops wearing the full veil after a police check, toward the end of 2017. She relates her turn away from the niqab:

With my face uncovered life changes, my life has become completely different. When you wear the jilbab, it's much less brutal, less violent, whereas with the sitar life was stopped. It's true that I'm glad to be able to move around again, to take the subway and go shopping. But it's not a victory or a liberation to have taken off the sitar. I have a strange feeling of being stripped. For such a long time I thought that the niqab was mandatory because I was often with sisters who thought so. My husband doesn't share that opinion and thinks that the niqab is only a recommendation. I don't know anymore. What made me take it off was the police. But not just that, because also I had to find an apartment. I haven't gotten public housing yet and for me I can't imagine wearing it again right now. I'll wear it again when I have housing.

It's also because I'm scared of seeing my son taken away because I'm against vaccines and medicines. I refuse to get him vaccinated. If I had a daughter I'd be more worried because I'd have to teach her the necessity of wearing the veil. And that would be hard with society. Once a woman saw me wearing the jilbab with my son and said, "poor child, to have to grow up like that." But I don't care, I'm trying to be positive.

Manon invites me over several times for a snack, always seeking social connections, but time constraints mean I decline each time. When I finally try to reach her again, neither her telephone number nor her email address is working. She has disappeared into thin air, as do a large part of my set of women when they decide to start a new life. We could hazard that the niqab is a transitional period.

LINA

Parents of Moroccan Origin

Lina contacts me the day I publish an essay in *The Conversation* about women who have stopped wearing the niqab (January 30, 2018). The essay portrays an amalgamation of Alexia* and Hanane.* Lina says that she was touched by their stories. She is twenty-eight years old and asks me to listen to her testimony. I cannot verify it, not having met her, but it seems realistic to me. It is included here because it represents a relatively rare case of marital dependency.

Lina was born in 1989 to parents of Moroccan origin, born in Morocco but having arrived in France as children. She lives in Grenoble. The story of her life is similar to Naïma's;* she is manipulated by her husband, with whom she has lived for a long time—a lasting union of the kind that is fairly rare among niqab wearers. We find the same themes: an attraction to beauty and fashion, and then a break, the niqab, a closing-off, family neurosis.

The Niqab

At the very beginning, I started wearing the niqab because I lost my twin sister in a car accident. I thought it might help me. But my husband exploited it and it didn't work out like I wanted.

Before I was totally worldly. I was a model, beauty was my career. I met my husband through a girlfriend who knew him. He was a local guy. I wasn't interested in Arabs so fortunately he was Italian. He wasn't Muslim yet. He observed Ramadan, like everyone in my neighborhood. But our meeting happened too fast, love at first sight. After our marriage at city hall, he started to get interested in Islam. He said: why won't you wear the veil? When we met, I would wear short shorts and he would talk to me about modesty, etc. People stopped understanding. My girlfriends used to go out with me. Now I'm all alone in the world. I only needed him and Allah. Then I got pregnant and then I got pregnant again. We met in 2010 and married in 2011. I wore the jilbab for a month and then went straight to the niqab in 2012, when I was twenty-three.

Her Spouse

My husband is a pietist, he's not interested in current events. He doesn't understand me when I read the newspaper or watch the news. For him it's just brainwashing. In terms of religion he does what they tell him and

takes what he wants. My husband has changed his friend group. Before
he had friends like anyone else, then he started going to the mosque and
told me, we're going to follow the minhaj salafi. He went to Saudi
Arabia for the hajj. Before coming back he told me to wear the niqab.
After that we closed off, we had to keep to ourselves. We couldn't speak to
non-Salafi. He just disparaged everything, even though in Islam you're
not supposed to.

He grew a beard and wears serouel, the cropped pants that he fought
to wear at work. He's a train conductor for the SNCF. He took his work
pants and shortened them. He never wanted to cut his beard to go to
work but he agreed to. He's a world-class manipulator, he has the world
eating out of his hand. After work he puts on the quamis.

The hardest part was with my family but he got them on his side too.
He presents himself like he's a respectable person. He tried to marry
another woman but he didn't succeed. My parents took his side because
he told them that I'd take off the veil and that I was seeing men. When
I wanted to defend myself my parents didn't believe me. He played the
victim so much that he convinced everyone. At the beginning his mother
was on my side, she said that I was right to take off the veil and then he
said I'd cheated on him. He wins over everyone. He blames me for my
old job as a model and calls me a whore. He always tells me, I made
you what you are today. But he's never made me a happy woman.

The Law and the Niqab

*The law is what pushed me towards wearing the niqab. It had a big
influence on me. Why did they ban it? It seems like it was so that women
would want to wear it. I felt powerful under the niqab, above the law. At
first you feel like you're free, superior to others. But after that it gets hard.
You're constantly insulted and afraid of being assaulted. I wasn't ready. I
was brainwashed. Then when I came to my senses, I hated it. I wore the
niqab for ten months, almost a year, but it was so hard! Then I was
wearing the jilbab again and it was easier even if people called me Batman.
I was unhappy, I wasn't myself. It was so hard, I'd come home in tears.
Going from high fashion to that! I couldn't take it.*

*I got assaulted in the street. It was the street kids and the prostitutes
who defended me. I remember a little Black woman who was hooking,
she threatened an old guy who was yelling at me and chased him off.
I thanked her. Lots of the neighborhood youths defend me and I think
about them fondly. I knew several other women who wore the niqab but*

they didn't go out. Clearly they'd all started wearing the niqab after the law. Some of them stopped because they couldn't stand the violence against them. When I wanted to stop I realized that some of the sisters wearing the niqab thought they were above the others. They aren't educated, they have very little knowledge, but they overpower everyone. They think they're superior to others because they defy the law, they're above everything.

After the Niqab

My daughter asked me, why can't you come with me to the library? That broke my heart. I wanted to do things with my children, to share in their pleasures. It was a realization. My husband was disgusted when I stopped wearing the niqab. He beat me and called me a whore. He put so much pressure that in the end I even hated the jilbab. He insulted me when I went out without gloves even in the middle of summer. In the winter, he didn't want me to put a coat over my jilbab because he said they could see my body. I was cold—I only weigh 105 pounds. He said that I was a rebel and that in another country I'd be stoned. I don't love him at all anymore. I have no attraction to him, especially since he's gained fifty pounds. I hate him for all that he put me through. He's turned me off of modesty. Today I've taken it all off and separated from him. But it was very hard to get out.

CLAIRE

Convert to Islam

Figure 25. Claire filmed in Villiers-sur-Marne, summer 2013.

Claire is sixteen when we meet for the first time on June 30, 2013, at the Tawhid Mosque in Saint-Denis. She is coming to the funeral-washing class offered by the sisters there and is the only fully-veiled woman. She introduces herself as having converted two months ago and having worn the niqab for nine months, starting in October 2012. She is extremely mature for her age.

Profile

Born in 1997, Claire converted to Islam at age fourteen, in 2011. She briefly describes her parents as not liking Islam. With clarity, she describes her conversion process as a reaction against her family. She tells me she spent a year and a half not really practicing and then joined the *salafiyya*. She appreciates the *salafiyya*'s level of Islamic scholarship but faults their bad behavior. When I meet her, she has been Tablighi for four and a half months. She admits that the Tablighi don't have the same level of scholarship but admires their better behavior. The movement fulfills what she has always sought: a spirit of generosity toward others, without devoting something only to yourself. She combines *salafiyya* and Tablighi, taking what, in her opinion, is the best from each. She rejects the kind of sectarianism that leads to insular thinking. On the other hand, she is ferociously opposed to the "soufists [soufis] who are all over."

She recounts having been kicked out of her home and going to live in a shelter in Villiers. Her father is a police chief in the Paris suburbs. Her mother works in a bank, but she is no longer in contact with her. Her father has accepted her conversion to Islam but not her practice, even though she attempted to win him over with bandanas, headbands, etc.

When she receives her first fine for wearing the niqab in 2013, she says she did not attempt to have it annulled by her father: "Because we're opposed to the law in favor of religion, we have to accept the consequences and not cheat." She agrees to speak on camera, seeming almost eager for media attention to amplify her speech. She wants to be heard and express herself.

Later, I meet her at the entrance to the RER E at the Gare du Nord station, where she is slightly panicked. She has just taken off her niqab, pulling her jilbab over her nose when she notices the police:

> When I see police officers, I automatically take off my veil so as not to provoke them. You have to trust God and make your choices based on personal belief. I've been stopped a dozen times and fined three times, and the fines got sent to my father because I'm a minor.

Claire has been forbidden to wear a long skirt at school, which led her to become even more invested in Islam, her differentialist feeling reinforced by the high visibility. Her remarks are symptomatic of the niqab as a response to society's stigmatization of Islam. She returns to the influence of the law on her choice to wear the niqab:

> The law is what drove me to wear the niqab. If there hadn't been the law, I wouldn't even have worn the headscarf. If I hadn't been kicked out of school because of my long skirt, I would never have worn the niqab. I converted and started wearing the jilbab and then the niqab, a logical development. I started wearing the full veil as the law was being passed. I did research on the Internet, I read opinions for and against it and then I made my decision. My problems with my parents started way before my conversion to Islam.
>
> What's stupid about the law is that at first it only applied to a couple hundred women and now you see sitars everywhere in the mosques. I converted five years ago, at the time of the law. The niqab was almost non-existent. Some women wear the veil for strictly religious reasons, others to raise their self-esteem and to say: I'm stronger than the law.

Claire believes that the niqab was something already nascent in her that the law only brought to the surface. She thinks that the political context brought to light the expression of buried feeling. The law led her to the full veil, corresponding to the expression of her deepest being. She is glad about it: the lawmakers seeking to eradicate a phenomenon have instead become its propagandists.

I go with her on November 18, 2013, to the police station in Saint-Maur where she has been summoned. As soon as we exit the RER station, she adjusts her niqab and lowers the veil of the sitar over her eyes. Claire seems anxious, worried about confrontation. She hesitates between leaving on or taking off her niqab. She decides to keep it on: "I'm wearing it because that's what I was summoned for." She takes a deep breath as if to gather her courage and show her determination. She gives her identification at the entrance, raising the veil, and then lowers it to wait. At this moment, the woman at the entrance, in her forties and very curt, orders her to obey the law. Claire refuses, retorting that she has just arrived for the summons and that she will say nothing on her lawyer's advice (she is represented gratis by the CCIF [Collectif contre l'islamophie en France, or French Collective against Islamophobia], which she took the initiative to call before her appointment, who advised silence when she is not accompanied by her legal representatives).

At her exit, Claire recounts that she was not questioned about the niqab but "flattered" by a woman who offered her a coffee, using niceness to convince her to see a psychiatrist and remove the veil.

In February of 2015, I reestablish contact with her. She is one month past her eighteenth birthday. She was married in May of 2014. When I ask her about her studies, she says her goal is medicine and she wants to earn her professional diploma for "Support and Home Care Services." She thinks she will be able to practice medicine after that, to guide her toward midwife training the next year. She has since quit the nursing assistant training that she said she was taking, as she has the funeral-washing training at Saint-Denis where we first met, which didn't suit her.

She has returned to live with her father and has a good relationship with her mother, who reestablished contact. She insists that it was her mother, not herself, who first broke off ties. She affirms that she still wears the niqab even though she knows she will have to unveil her face in medical school.

She speaks of her relationship to others:

I'm most scared of people's insults and violence. I go by police in the street every day without being stopped. But the insults are constant. People in public yell at me. That's why I chose not to go out anymore. In the train I always hear people saying, "Go back to your country." It's

> maddening! I'm French! I even got told that I was being paid by Saudi Arabia. Once a man told me, "You turn me on with your full veil." That was harassment. I wanted to file a complaint to the transportation police but they did nothing. What's happening is awful, France is more and more like a dictatorship. It's scary when you see what the country is becoming.

I lose contact with her at the beginning of 2016 and at first do not know how to reach her. After a two-year break, I reach out to her again in February of 2018. I start by contacting her father at the police station, but he never responds, and I give up. Finally, I find her Facebook account, with her real name. She responds immediately. She is twenty-one years old and has two daughters, born in 2016 and 2017. She tells me that she stopped wearing the niqab at the beginning of 2016 and goes by her original first name, and not her converted name. She describes herself as a childcare assistant, in addition to taking care of her own children, aged two and fifteen months. She still hopes to travel to Africa for humanitarian work. Today she wears only the jilbab:

> I didn't find my place wearing the niqab. I took it off myself. I'm still practicing, I've found a way of doing it that works for me. I'm much more at peace with myself. I had difficult times, I was denying my emotions. I need to find myself and to re-center myself. I think a lot about that time at the Saint-Maur station. It was a call for help. I was uncomfortable in my skin and in my religion, even if I acted proud.

Very interested in her post-niqab perspective, I ask her a series of questions. As before, her responses are very clear:

> At the time, I was competitive about my appearance. I wore the sitar for others, not myself. In middle and high school I was bullied by the other girls. My parents put me in a different school and I lost my friends. I landed in a private middle school where it was worse, I was still bullied. I didn't have any friends at all and needed to belong to a group. At the beginning, my conversion to Islam came out of needing to belong to a group, even if after it also became sincere. I was bullied by Muslim girls: they were frustrated, they saw the people putting them down in me, everyone who refused to give them jobs, everyone who criticizes North Africans. My idea was to show that I was like them. I was so alone and it's hard to be alone when you're a teenager. After I converted I met other sisters. At first it was just to find friends but it was never enough. The only way I found was to wear the full veil and go to the mosque. With the niqab I was like them.

I understand why kids go to Syria—school bullying is so strong. Others do shamanic travel to go get high. They're the type of loners who need to belong to a group. When you wear the niqab you're automatically friends with people like you. I wore the sitar very young, for three years. Everyone around me was wearing it. I converted in that atmosphere and for me it was normal. I never imagined you could wear anything but the jilbab. But I never understood the women who wore the niqab with eye makeup. If you want to hide yourself, why would you want to accentuate the only visible part of your body? And then with the ablutions, the makeup runs.

I stopped wearing it because I wasn't living anymore. I don't regret having worn the niqab because I understood things but I don't want to put it back on. The women who wear it today wear it for Allah but they're very rare. The others have given up. The women stop wearing it because they're afraid: afraid of being assaulted and afraid of being lumped in with people on the government's watchlist and with ISIS.

Today I'm fighting other fights: breastfeeding and home birth, healthier fights. I'm also fighting against obstetrical violence. When a woman does anything, people feel like they have to judge her. Women are always wrong, whether it's that their skirts are too short or too long or they wear the veil. Men should have no say on the veil or on obstetrical violence. The act of thinking in the place of women is antifeminism.

The Niqab: Refuting Common Ideas

After a year and a half of controversy, the passage of the ban law in France led a nearly unanimous condemnation of the niqab. This condemnation was based on clichés about Muslim women: submission to their husbands, imprisonment at home, domestic violence. But reality contradicts these preconceptions. Niqab wearers are predominantly single or divorced women, independent, and dominant in their relationships.

It is worth spending time demystifying some of the clichés about women who wear the niqab that are rooted in public opinion. Supporters of the ban in France were effective in building aversion to the niqab across social strata. What these individuals had in common was that they had never met the women who were the object of their discourse.

Let us examine some of these commonplaces:

1. The niqab arrived in France via immigration

Many French citizens believe that women who veil their faces come from Muslim countries where the niqab is customary. But the niqab in Western countries is not a matter of parental heritage; on the contrary, it is worn in opposition to the family and the traditional veil. The full veil can give these young women a reason to leave their families and, paradoxically, to break with tradition (Salafi could be seen as an anti-tradition). The majority of the Salafi studied here correspond to this profile: they are from acculturated families and discover religion later in life. The niqab is linked to a realization of the self and a return to faith. Its wearing is based on a new model of society and the construction of a new woman, in charge of her life—the opposite, in some ways, of the veil worn by the first immigrants.

2. Niqab wearers disrespect the customs of their host country

Those who believe that the niqab has come to France from elsewhere (in general) believe that its wearers, who are therefore immigrants, make no effort to integrate themselves into the society in which they live. Furthermore, they perceive all veils, whether the hijab or the niqab, as traditional, leading to a feeling of "invasion" by a foreign culture, a sort of "reverse colonization." Niqab wearers are often subject to the same phrase: "go back to your country." Yet almost all of them are French citizens. Converts to Islam make up almost half of women in the full veil. All of them speak French perfectly.

3. The niqab is a sign of Muslim communitarianism

A classic argument against whoever claims a distinctive Muslim cultural or religious identity, communitarianism is brandished to describe the threat that these women might represent. And yet many niqab wearers, operating according to an elitist logic, prefer to distinguish themselves from other Muslim women who practice a "cultural" Islam. In other words, they reject this supposed Muslim communitarianism. The Salafi promote an Islam purged of customs that they perceive as *bid'ah* (blameworthy innovation) and are thus opposed to the "community" whose practices they reject.

And yet, the law has also led to a new form of communitarianism. Prevented from accessing public services, women have had to turn to the men of their "community"—in other words, a network of practicing Muslims, held together by the mosque, to do their errands and drive them by car. The same phenomenon was produced by the passage of the ban in 2004 (the ban of religious symbols in public schools), which led young girls kept out of schools to seek religious education. Muslim middle and high schools, which might be loosely seen to be linked to "communitarianism," were born out of the 2004 law.[9] It might thus be said that the communitarianism, vilified by politicians, is one of the consequences of the will to eradicate visible signs of Islam, driving students to prefer a more truly community-minded education.

Still today, when they are not homeschooling, many niqab wearers with children send them to private Muslim schools that appeared after the ban on religious symbols in 2004, thereby limiting their exchanges to within the Muslim community—a behavior termed as communitarianism that the French government has said it seeks to combat but only encourages and has in fact provoked. Although the majority of French Muslims were initially against the niqab, police intervention has pushed them to solidarity with their "sisters." The law has had a negative impact on Muslims as a whole (across the spectrum and including integrated or entirely assimilated Muslims strongly opposed to the niqab), who see it as a measure against Islam in light of the tiny number of women concerned, which encourages them to come together under a common Muslim identity.[10]

4. Niqab wearers are forced to veil themselves by fathers, brothers, or husbands

For the niqab's opponents, the women who wear it embody the figure of the victim, consenting or not, of a repressive patriarchal system that forces them into social disappearance. This reclusion of the female body is seen to be mandated by men. Women's capacity to act is denied on the pretext that women are under the control of a male family member who uses the veil to coerce her, keeping her face for himself alone.

And yet, often in the case of the niqab wearer, the father is absent. Women often come from broken families. Women who wear the niqab are not acting in obedience to their families; on the contrary, they react against them or seek revenge. It is also the case that women wearing the niqab are rarely married or in relationships. The majority of them are single; some of them are young women who have never been married, while others are divorced after one or several short marriages. Married women wearing the niqab have primarily entered into Salafi as they have returned to religion, an ideology chosen by both members of the couple or by the woman herself. I have not met women who were forced to wear the niqab by men, an observation confirmed by the niqab wearers in my study, whom I systematically asked about this possibility.

5. Niqab wearers are forbidden from leaving home

The idea of women being kept in their homes by their husbands is often raised as an objection by those who argue that niqab wearers are the victims of domestic coercion. My response to this argument is that if women did not leave their house, they would not wear the niqab. They would thus not be part of my study. The niqab is linked to women's entry into public spaces. But we do see, in the cases of Naïma* and Lina,* that a husband might use the law prohibiting the niqab in public spaces to lock up and psychologically torture his wife.

6. Niqab wearers are submissive

Public opinion holds that niqab wearers are passive and lack wills of their own. On the contrary: niqab wearers are often strong-willed, confronting both their friends and family and public condemnation, often on their own. They can even be domineering, imposing their will on those around them. The niqab can force its wearer's husband into strict obedience to Islamic rules, such as mosque going, abstaining from alcohol, and casual sexual encounters. Few men agree to the required lifestyle, and many choose to leave.

Moreover: why should the niqab be a sign of submission? Nothing in the history of facial veiling suggests that the practice diminishes the veil-wearer. Instead, hiding one's identity is the mark of a superhero, or a member of the black bloc, or a burglar. Some niqab wearers enhance their images, taking selfies and creating Facebook pages.

7. The niqab is a prison

The idea of prison has been repeatedly used by detractors of the facial veil, most notably by the communist representative André Gerin, a proponent of the law, through his pronouncement that "The burqa is a walking prison"[11] on June 17, 2009. Safiya contests this:

> *In no way are we in prison. Prison means bars, being deprived of freedom. People don't come see us at home. I have no bars on my windows and when I go out in my niqab it doesn't have bars. I go out whenever I want.*

Soraya,* even, reverses the cliché of the prison to describe her feeling of freedom:

> *Maybe others see it as a prison but actually I've never felt so free in my life.*

In Europe (excluding the UK), wearing the niqab is a voluntary step undertaken by independent women, free in their movements and generally going out alone (rarely accompanied by a man). Cases like Naïma's* and Lina's* are rare.

8. The burqa is a sign of Islam's oppression of women

This accusation extends beyond the niqab to encompass all veils worn by Muslim women, although it is exponentially stronger when the veil covers the face as well. Even though we have seen that, in France, niqab wearers are rarely married and generally act on their own will, opponents respond that even unmarried, these women have interiorized their own inferiority and alienation compared to men. The idea of women acting against their own interests is widespread.

This ideological construction is so prevalent in public opinion that it has sparked a kind of "backward thinking" that extends to and misinterprets everything related to Islam, mixing registers and contexts. Afghanistan or Saudi Arabia are invoked, for example, when speaking of the niqab in Europe. These are bad arguments: the obligatory burqa in Afghanistan is not the same as the niqab worn voluntarily in the West while banned by law. Whereas wearing the former is normative and conformist, the latter is anti-normative and anti-conformist, as Safiya emphasizes:

> *There women are forced to wear it and here they want to force us to take it off. So I still see some similarities. It's a dictatorship.*

This is also the reason Amnesty International has condemned both the mandatory wearing of the full veil under the Taliban and the bans in Europe and Denmark as "a discriminatory violation of women's rights," in violation of "the rights to freedom of expression and freedom of religion."[12]

In Europe (again with the exception of the UK), the niqab is the manifestation of a desire to transgress norms. Niqab wearers choose of their own volition to wear it. And yet the public continues to see Islam as a monolithic block, lumping together all practices of veiling for women. In reality, such practices are polysemic and multiform.

9. The niqab is misogynistic and oppressive

The attribution of negative moral values to this article of clothing is also largely widespread in European populations, who have difficulty imagining that the full veil could have other meanings. To oppose the niqab to gender equality is another way of devaluing or dismissing Islam and essentializing it as a "misogynist" religion.

But the women who join the Salafi do not consider the fundamental texts of Islam misogynist. Instead, they find in the various interpretations of these texts, multiple advantages in terms of self-esteem and personal valorization, not to mention valuing them simply as symbols of their faith. A first cursory talk with a woman wearing a jilbab or niqab might seem to demonstrate her narcissistic satisfaction in the clothing she wears, but it is still necessary to speak with these women.

10. The niqab goes against equality of the sexes

The argument that Islam promotes inequality between the sexes is another Western projection and the legacy of orientalism. The Moroccan feminist Asma Lamrabet has brilliantly debunked many clichés surrounding women's purported inferiority in Islam, including those that originate in the Muslim world. Women who wear the niqab, or even the veil, do not feel inferior to men; on the contrary, they take up positions of control and choice. To live with one's face veiled can produce a feeling of superiority, of being above others, due to an escape from social standards of beauty and etiquette. There is perhaps a rejection of equality on the part of these women, but not in the commonly acknowledged sense—instead, they see themselves as superior. Of course, this might be a technique used by religious leaders to alienate women and give them an illusion of power that they will not possess, but in the French context, these women largely live alone and are under no control except for their own.

Additionally, the Salafi are sometimes accused of promoting a separation between the sexes that is supposedly against French values. Yet Europe has a long tradition of separation that still runs strong. Masonic temples, for example, were primarily reserved for men. The Rotary Club only began to admit women in 1989. The Catholic clergy is also exclusively male, and high-level sports are strictly separated by sex.

11. Niqab wearers must be freed even against their will

The idea of freeing Muslims who have interiorized their own inferiority has not changed for over two decades, starting with the first headscarf controversy in 1989. The 2010 law was introduced as helping "free women." Some pronouncements, collected and filmed from the National Assembly representatives (July 7–13, 2010): "The law will be useful to free women, to free young girls in certain neighborhoods where their lives are hellish" (André Gerin, PC); "[These are] women the Republic cannot abandon even if there were only one, even if she has marginalized herself voluntarily" (Jean-François Copé, UMP); "It's a movement—and it's not going to stop with just the veil—that involves the ghettoization of women, a sort of dhimmitude [sic] of women, or in other words an inferior status" (Jacques Myard, UMP).[13] This "liberation of Muslim women" is described by American scholar Lila Abu Lughod in her book entitled *Do Muslim Women Need Saving?*[14]

12. Niqab wearers support polygamy

The case of Sandrine Moulères, fined in 2010 for her niqab, sparked a controversy when the media revealed that her husband, Lies Hebbadj, had seventeen children with four different wives. Admittedly, some niqab or jilbab wearers agree to a religious marriage with a married man and to have one or several co-wives. They even see value in it, able to identify with the mythologized model of Muhammad's wives. Some of them also have more self-interested reasons—for example, to be able to undertake the *hegira*, in the case of Saliha,* who leaves for Syria via Tataouine after having married an already-married Frenchman over social media, so he can receive her there. These women, in a non-Muslim context, are the equivalent of the mistresses of powerful men, which would not at all be shocking in France. Even if the "official" discourse of Salafi women seems tolerant of polygamous unions, it is rare that they are so tolerant in reality. Other women are fiercely opposed to polygamy. Samia,* for example:

> *In my religion the man has the right to marry four wives. But I don't like that right. I don't respect it. If it happened to me I'd get a divorce. I'm not giving him the chance to marry someone else. Impossible. I don't want anything like that.*

13. Niqab wearers are in a cult

Those who refuse to engage Salafi women express the same aversion they would have toward members of a cult: they are not to be spoken to because they have abandoned their status as an autonomous subject. The same goes for Muslims in general, who are suspected of being subject to some control that is beyond them. They are under the power of an imam or a manipulative husband, for example, and so dominated that they are no longer in charge of their own existence, but are agents of a patriarchal order, forcing them to cover themselves completely. The comparison between Salafi and cults returns, indeed, frequently in the writings of critics and even scholars.

Olivier Roy writes of the theory of "brainwashing" that lets parents explain the choices of their daughters who have converted, when in reality these women are emancipated and modern.[15] Yet, even if we can understand the feelings of parents who become desperate after their daughters' departures for Syria, such empathy is irrelevant for criticism or scholarship. Niqab wearers are subjects who speak and think, capable of reflecting on the reasons behind their actions, with self-awareness that is completely clear. These women are not powerless but are subjects in their own right.

14. The niqab is not in the Quran and therefore not Muslim

Several figures, speaking during the debates before the ban was passed, asserted that the Quran does not say the full veil is required and thus it is not a religious obligation. Politicians, philosophers, journalists, and the media provided the French public (Muslims included) with lessons in Islam to show that the niqab is neither "Muslim" nor "Quranic."

Some individuals, such as Michèle Alliot-Marie,[16] objected that Muslim women cannot veil their faces in Mecca. They concluded that the niqab is not a religious requirement. This is another instance of absurd thinking. Sandrine Moulères, the only French niqab wearer to write a book about her experience, counters it easily:

> Using the Prophet's words as recounted by Ibn Omar, some politicians tried to claim that women don't wear the veil even in Mecca. The phrase they cite is: "The woman takes off her niqab in the state of sacralization [during the turns around the *Kaaaba*]." This is true. But if she takes it off, then she's wearing it normally, isn't she?[17]

We might also object that politicians such as Alliot-Marie are breaking the 1905 law separating church and state; certainly, they are not charged with giving theological advice to Muslims.

Acknowledgments

This book is written in memory of my father, Tullio, to whom I owe my interest in religious customs.

My thanks, first and foremost, to all the women, more than 200 of them, who confided their innermost thoughts and most private experiences to me. Despite their fears of being instrumentalized—for they are regularly the target of caricaturing attacks and articles—they allowed me to collect their stories here. I hope they will forgive me for having revealed some of their confidences. My goal has been to humanize them, allowing the public to better understand them, all while protecting their anonymity and keeping to myself any secrets revealed by women whose identities have become public.

My most sincere thanks as well to Michel Wieviorka, my former thesis director at the EHESS (École des hautes etudes en sciences sociales) in Paris, and also to Jean Baubérot, Nilüfer Göle, Farhad Khosrokhavar, Raphaël Liogier, and Alain Policar. I want to express my deepest gratitude to Olivier Roy, whose work strongly influenced my research and who understood the importance of my work on the full veil in 2006.

Thanks to Marc Rozenblum, my husband, who supported me unfailingly. In addition to his multiple re-readings of the text, he accompanied me without hesitation when I needed to talk to senior Tablighi officials in India and Salafi activists in Tunis.

And finally, thanks to Thomas Lay of Fordham University Press for being inspired to publish my book in English and to Lindsay Turner for her wonderful translation, made with great finesse and intelligence.

Notes

A Note on Terminology

1. [Translator's note: this is the law prohibiting all face-covering garments in France.]
2. [Translator's note: While the construction "niqabée" makes sense in French, in the English text I have chosen to use "niqab wearers" or "women who wear the niqab," which preserves the sense of agency De Féo emphasizes even if it requires more words.]
3. John Tolan, *Faces of Muhammad: Western Perceptions of the Prophet of Islam from the Middle Ages to Today* (Princeton: Princeton University Press, 2019).

Introduction

1. The controversy was seen to begin with Nicolas Sarkozy's June 2009 declaration that "the niqab is not welcome in France." The commission in question is fact-finding commission number 2262, led by André Gerin (Community Party, mayor of the Vénissieux suburb of Lyon) and assisted by Éric Raoult (UMP).
2. [Translator's note: Wearing a facial covering is the equivalent of a second-class driving offense. French driving citations are divided into five classes, the first being a simple traffic violation (no fine) and the fifth being exceeding the speed limit by over 50 km/h, with a fine of up to 3,000 euros.]
3. Amnesty International, "L'interdiction du voile est contraire aux droits humains" ["Banning the Veil is a Violation of Human Rights"], *Le Fil*, (August/September 2010): 40:4.
4. "Une instance de l'Onu demande à la France de réviser sa loi contre le voile intégral" ["A UN Committee Asks France to Review its Law Against the Full-Face Veil"], lemonde.fr, October 23, 2018.

5. For instance: Al-Haramayn, Al-Azhar, Maison d'Ennour, Orientica, Sana, and Al-Bouraq editions. Today this kind of business also exists in the Paris suburbs, such as Maison d'Ennour in Aubervilliers.

6. See the documentaries by Agnès De Féo, produced by Marc Rozenblum (Sasana Productions): *Mission Tabligh* (2009), about the Tablighi movement in Southeast Asia (Malaysia, Cambodia, Indonesia); *Sous la burqa* (2010) and *Niqab Hors-la-loi* (2012) in the context of the French Salafi movement exclusively; *Au Cœur de Deoband* (2011); and *Niqabmania à Tunis* (2013) on the full veil in India and post-revolutionary Tunisia; as well as *La Tunisie et ses femmes salafistes* (2015) published on lemonde.fr on May 22, 2015. Again, in the context of France, see *Émilie König vs Ummu Tawwab* (2016), published on the *L'Obs* website on May 12, 2016, and republished on *Slate* on January 3, 2018. The eighth of De Féo's films, *Voile interdit* (2017), also takes up the various laws banning veils for women and their effects on the Muslim population.

7. [Translator's note: according to this convention, childless women are sometimes given the honorific (or *kunya*) "Oum" placed before the name of an abstract virtue, object, or quality that characterizes or is associated with that woman.]

8. Barbara Metcalf, "Tablîghî Jamâ'at and Women," in *Travellers in Faith: Studies of the Tablîghî Jamâ'at as a Transnational Islamic Movement for Faith Renewal*, ed. Muhammad Khalid Masud (Leiden: Brill, 2000), 44–58.

9. The term *manhaj* is prevalent in Salafi vocabulary: Saliha's* former email address, for example, is soeursminhaj@hotmail.com [manhaj sisters].

10. Mohamed Achamlane's nickname, Cortex, comes from the French translation of Steven Spielberg's cartoon "Pinky and the Brain" ("Minus et Cortex" in French). The show was broadcast in France starting in 1996. The group's first members adopted this name for their leader before opting for the more Islamic "Abou Hamza."

11. My footage from this rally was included in two documentaries, *Niqab Hors-la-loi* (2012) and *Émile König vs Ummu Tawwab* (2016), since König had attempted to join Forsane Alizza. The group's inclusion in the first documentary would lead to several disputes with its subjects, some of whom demanded to be removed so as not to be associated with Forsane Alizza. Only Naïma* supports the group today; all the other women included strongly condemn their actions.

12. [Translator's note: the phrase used in French is "les Français de-souche, les sous-chiens." The phrase "de souche" means "native" or "blueblood." The word "sous-chiens," or "Souchiens," is a play on words for people who are "de souche." "Souchiens" is aurally identical to "sous-chiens," or "less than dogs." (In fact, a French anti-racist activist, Houria Boutelja, was taken to French court in late 2011, accused of "anti-white racism" for using the phrase, which was said to evoke the Nazi epithet "sous-hommes." She was acquitted in early 2012.)]

13. Imam, an association leader of Tunisian origin who presents himself as a supporter of the French government, often appearing in the media for his anti-Islamist and republican positions.

14. Former rector of the Paris Mosque.

The Sociology of Niqab Wearers

1. Nilüfer Göle, *Interpénétrations: L'Islam et l'Europe* (Paris: Galaade Éditions, 2005), 72.
2. Olivier Roy, *Jihad and Death: The Global Appeal of the Islamic State*, trans. Cynthia Schoch (Oxford: Oxford University Press, 2017), 42.
3. Malika El Aroud, *Soldats de lumière* (.pdf, Ansar al-Haqq website, 2003), 11.
4. Sandrine Moulères, *Les boucs émissaires de la République: Moi, Sandrine, ma vie, mon histoire, ma vérité* (Paris: Michalon, 2010), 96.
5. Olivier Roy, *Secularism Confronts Islam*, trans. George Holoch (New York: Columbia University Press, 2007).
6. Sandrine Moulères, *Les boucs émissaires de la République*.
7. Article 224-4-10 of French law number 2010-1192, October 11, 2020: "The act of any person forcing one or several other people to hide their face, through threat, violence, coercion, abuse of authority or abuse of power, in reason of their sex, is punishable by one year in prison and a fine of 30,000 euros. If the act is committed in the case of a minor, the penalty is raised to two years in prison and a fine of 60,000 euros," legifrance.gouv.fr.
8. Agnès De Féo, "After the Niqab: What Life is Like for French Women Who Remove the Veil," trans. Leighton Walter Kille, theconversation.com, February 26, 2018.
9. These examples of Arabic sayings come from the Facebook account Niqab Lovers.
10. Jean-Claude Kaufmann, *Corps de femmes, regards d'hommes: Sociologie des seins nus [Women's Bodies, Men's Gazes: Sociology of Bare Breasts]* (Paris: Pocket, "Agora" collection, 1998 [1995]).
11. Adih El Qarni, *Soyez la femme la plus heureuse au monde [Be the Happiest Woman in the World]*, trans. Ahmad ben Saghir ben Mohammed (Riyadh: IIPH Editions, 2012).
12. Examples of classic Salafi "masters of thought" translated into French or English include: Al Albani, *Le voile de la femme musulmane*, summarized by Husam Al-Din Afana (Lyon-Paris: Dar Al Muslim, 2007); Abd Al-Munim Salim Amr, ed., *Recueil de fatwas concernant les femmes: Ibn Bâz, Al-Albânî, Ibn Uthaymin* (Brussels: Al Hadith, 2011); and Muhammad Ibn Ahmed Ibn Ismail, *The Veil: Evidence of Niqab* (London: Al-Firdous Editions, 2009).
13. Olivier Roy, *Secularism Confronts Islam*, 74.
14. Maryam Atiya, *Faux hadiths au sujet de la femme [False Hadiths Concerning Women]* (Lyon: Tawhid, 2013).
15. Asma Lamrabet, *Femmes et hommes dans le Coran: Quelle égalité? [Equality? Women and Men in the Quran]* (Paris: Albouraq, 2012); *Croyantes et féministes: Un autre regard sur les religions [Believers and Feminists: A New Look at Religions]* (Paris: Albouraq, 2017).
16. Amr Abd Al-Munim Salim, ed., *Recueil des fatwas concernant les femmes [Collection of Fatwas About Women]* (al-Hadith, 2011), 292.

The Niqab and the Other

1. Sandrine Moulères, *Les boucs émissaires de la République: Moi, Sandrine, ma vie, mon histoire, ma vérité* (Paris: Michalon, 2010), 115–116.
2. Agnès De Féo, "Le niqab, une revanche des femmes?" ["The Niqab: Women's Revenge?"], Slate.fr, October 11, 2016.
3. Jean-Claude Kaufmann, *La femme seule et le prince charmant: Enquête sur la vie en solo* [*The Single Woman and Prince Charming: A Study of the Single Life*] (Paris: Pocket, 2006 [1999]).
4. [Translator's note: the book, co-authored with William Hoffer, was published in the U.S. in 1987 and made into a movie starring Sally Field as its protagonist in 1991.]
5. Zeina and Djénane Kareh Tager, *Sous mon niqab: Je l'ai enlevé au péril de ma vie* [*Beneath My Niqab: I Risked my Life to Take it Off*] (Paris: Plon, 2010).
6. The journalist Djénane Kareh Tager specializes in co-writing these dramatized witness accounts by Muslim women.
7. [Translator's note: "Fantômas" refers to a well-known fictional French crime figure created in the early twentieth century who appeared as masked and sometimes cape-wearing on screen.]

A Reaction to the Ban

1. Shamsou, from Brussels: "I do it for me and for Allah *soubhana wa taala*, not for my parents or for the creators of this worldly life."
2. Naïma, from Aubervilliers: "The law against the niqab that was passed in 2010 led to a feeling of injustice. The most docile sheep just follow their government's path. As soon as they see a woman wearing the niqab in the street, as soon as they see me in the street, they shout, they insult me, stop me, tell me that it's banned."
3. Agnès De Féo, *Niqab Hors-la-loi*, Documentary, 2012.
4. De Féo, *Niqab Hors-la-loi*, 2012
5. De Féo, *Niqab Hors-la-loi*, 2012.
6. Rachid Nekkaz, *Le Voltaire du niqab* (Algeria: Mouvement pour la jeunesse et le changement, 2018).
7. Howard S. Becker, *Outsiders: Studies in the Sociology of Deviance* (New York: The Free Press, 2008 [1963]), 9.
8. Becker, *Outsiders*, 3.
9. Becker, *Outsiders*, 11.
10. Élisabeth Badinter, "Adresse à celles que portent volontairement la burqa" ["Address to Women Voluntarily Wearing the Burqa"], *Le Nouvel Observateur*, July 9, 2009.
11. Interview with Élisabeth Badinter, lemonde.fr, April 1, 2016.
12. Michel Wieviorka, *Retour au sens: Pour en finir avec le déclinisme* [*Returning to Sense: Ending Declinism*] (Paris: Robert Laffont, 2015), 92.

13. Raphaël Liogier, "Le voile intégral comme trend hypermoderne" ["The Full Veil as Hypermodern Trend"], *Multitudes* 42: 14–20.

14. Olivier Roy, *Secularism Confronts Islam*, trans. George Holoch (New York: Columbia University Press, 2007), 88.

15. Olivier Roy, *Jihad and Death: The Global Interpénétrations: L'Islam et l'Europe Appeal of the Islamic State*, trans. Cynthia Schoch (Oxford: Oxford University Press, 2017), 67.

16. Francis Dupuis-Déri, *Who's Afraid of the Black Blocks? Anarchy in Action Around the World*, trans. Lazer Lederhendler (Binghamton: PM Press, 2014).

17. David Le Breton, *Disparaître de soi: Une tentation contemporaine [Self-Disappearance: A Contemporary Temptation]* (Paris: Métailié, 2015), 25.

18. David Le Breton, *Corps et adolescence* (Brussels: yapaka.be, 2016), 38–39.

19. Agnès De Féo, *Niqabmania à Tunis*, Documentary, 2013.

Conclusion

1. David Le Breton, *Disparaître de soi: Une tentation contemporaine [Self-Disappearance: A Contemporary Temptation]* (Paris: Métailié, 2015), 25.

2. Olivier Roy, *Secularism Confronts Islam*, trans. George Holoch (New York: Columbia University Press, 2007), 89.

3. Maleiha Malik, "De la persecution des hérétiques à la loi sur le voile" ["From the persecution of heretics to the laws on the veil"], *Place publique*, September-October 2014: 75.

4. Olivier Roy, *Secularism Confronts Islam*, 104.

5. See the Amnesty International report, *Give us Respect and Justice! Overcoming Barriers to Justice for Women Rape Survivors*, March 5, 2019, the theme of which is "the culture of rape and impunity which benefits rapists exposed."

6. Véronique Le Goaziou, *Viol: Que fait la justice [Rape: What Constitutes Justice?]*, preface by Antoine Garapon (Paris: Presses de Sciences Po, 2019).

7. In French, veil (voile) and rape (viol) are almost homophones.

16 Portraits of Women Wearing the Niqab

1. [Translator's note: the French word for "fine" is "amende," which is similar to the French word for "almond," "amande."]

2. [Translator's note: "Belphegor" is a common name for a ghost or phantom, but the name here draws on the iconography of French cinema, referring to the character in *Phantom of the Louvre* (1965, remade in 2001, based on a 1927 novel by Arthur Bernède).]

3. [Translator's note: the officer uses the informal second-person pronoun "tu" rather than the formal "vous," which would commonly be used in respectful interactions with law enforcement.]

4. Aude Lorriaux, "Il faut regarder ce dialogue d'une femme en niqab et d'une touriste en colère à Nice" ["A Must-See Exchange between a Woman Wearing a Niqab and an Angry Tourist in Nice"], slate.fr, September 17, 2016.

5. I have chosen to omit Alexia's birthdate in order to protect her from any identification, even with her pseudonym.

6. Report by Saddek Chettab, "De Paris au Yémen: ces Français qui ont choisi l'islam radical" ["From Paris to Yemen: the French who Have Chosen Radical Islam"], *Enquête exclusive*, M6, November 20, 2011.

7. French-Algerian terrorist who carried out several attacks in the South of France that left seven dead in March 2012. He was shot dead by the police at the age of twenty-three.

8. Department in central France.

9. The first such establishment, Averroès high school, founded in Lille in 2003, precedes the law's passage but was nonetheless brought about by the controversy. Following this were Alif middle and high school in Toulouse in 2004, Al-Kindi middle and high school in the suburbs of Lyon in 2007, and Ibn Khaldoun middle school in Marseille in 2009. Since then, several dozen Muslim establishments have appeared in France.

10. This is also the argument made by sociologist Vincent Gessier: "Many Muslims, initially very hostile to the wearing of the niqab, have become sympathetic towards these girls because they feel collectively targeted." *Le Temps*, July 1, 2010.

11. "Le burqa, une 'prison ambulante'" ["The Burqa: a 'walking prison'"], interview with André Gerin, *Libération*, June 17, 2009.

12. Press release: "Denmark: the ban on garments hiding a women's face constitute a discriminatory violation of women's rights," May 31, 2018.

13. See the documentary *Voile interdit* (2017). See also Jacques Myard's proposed law aiming to combat violations of women's human dignity resulting from certain religious practices.

14. Lila Abu Lughod, *Do Muslim Women Need Saving?* (Cambridge: Harvard University Press, 2013).

15. Olivier Roy, *Jihad and Death: The Global Interpénétrations: L'Islam et l'Europe Appeal of the Islamic State*, trans. Cynthia Schoch (Oxford: Oxford University Press, 2017), 51.

16. Interview with Michèle Alliot-Marie, French Minister of Justice at the time, in *Le Parisien*, May 19, 2010, "Voile intégral: 'des États islamiques l'ont aussi banni'" ["Full Veil: 'Muslim Countries Have Also Banned It'"]: "It's even banned in Mecca." Remarks collected on the fact-checking blog Les Décodeurs, "Les inventions de Michèle Alliot-Marie sur le voile intégral à La Mecque" ["Michèle Alliot-Marie's Inventions About the Full Veil in Mecca"], lemonde.fr, May 19, 2010.

17. Sandrine Moulères, *Les boucs émissaires de la République: Moi, Sandrine, ma vie, mon histoire, ma vérité* (Paris: Michalon, 2010), 145–146.

Selected Bibliography and Filmography

Bibliography

Aboudrar, Bruno Nassim. *Comment le voile est devenu musulman*. Paris: Champs Essais Flammarion, 2017 [2014].
Adraoui, Mohamed-Ali. *Salafism Goes Global: From the Gulf to the French Banlieues*. Translated by Henry Randolph. Oxford: Oxford University Press, 2020.
Ali, Zahra, ed. *Féminismes islamiques*. Paris: La Fabrique, 2012.
Amghar, Samir. *Le salafisme aujourd'hui*. Paris: Michalon, 2011.
Baubérot, Jean. *La laïcité falsifiée*. Paris: La Découverte, 2012.
Becker, Howard S. *Outsiders: Studies in the Sociology of Deviance*. New York: Free Press of Glencoe, 1963.
Benslama, Fethi and Farhad Khosrokhavar. *Le jihadisme des femmes: Pourquoi ont-elles choisi Daech?* Paris: Le Seuil, 2017.
Chouder, Ismahane, Malika Latrèche, and Pierre Tevanian. *Les filles voilées parlent*. Paris: La Fabrique, 2008.
De Féo, Agnès. "De L'Asie du Sud-Est à la banlieue parisienne: filmer les femmes en 'burqua." *Eurasie* 20 (2010): 174-171.
———. "Le voile intégral en France." Revue *Socio* (2018): 135-158.
———. *Le voile intégral en perspective 2008-2019*. Doctoral dissertation in sociology, directed by Michel Wieviorka, École des hautes études en sciences sociales, Paris, 2019.
Delthombe, Thomas. *L'Islam imaginaire: La construction médiatique de l'islamophobie en France (1975-2005)*. Paris: La Découverte, 2005.
Dupuis-Déri, Francis. *Who's Afraid of the Black Blocks? Anarchy in Action Around the World*. Translated by Lazer Lederhendler. Binghamton: PM Press, 2014.
Gaspard, Françoise and Khosrokhavar. *Le foulard et la République*. Paris: La Découverte, 1995.

Godard, Bernard. *La question musulmane en France: Un état des lieux sans concessions.* Paris: Fayard, 2015.
Göle, Nilüfer. *Musulmanes et modernes: Voile et civilization en Turquie.* Paris: La Découverte, 1993.
——. *Interpénétrations: L'Islam et l'Europe.* Paris: Galaade Editions, 2005.
——. *The Daily Lives of Muslims: Islam and Public Confrontation in Contemporary Europe.* Translated by Jacqueline Lerescu. London: Zed Books, 2017.
Guénolé, Thomas. *Islamopsychose: Pourquoi la France diabolise les musulmans.* Paris: Fayard, 2017.
Hamidi, Malika. *Un féminisme musulman, et pourquoi pas?* L'Aube: La Tour d'Aigues, 2017.
Inge, Anabel. *The Making of a Salafi Muslim Woman: Paths to Conversion.* New York: Oxford University Press, 2017.
Kaufmann, Jean-Claude. *Corps de femmes, regards d'hommes: Sociologie des seins nus.* Paris: Pocket, Agora collection, 1998 [1995].
——. *The Single Woman and the Fairytale Prince.* Translated by David Macey. London: Polity Press, 2008.
Khedimellah, Moussa. "Jeunes prédicateurs du movement Tabligh." *Socio-anthropologie* 10 (2001).
Khosrokhavar, Farad. *Suicide Bombers: Allah's New Martyrs.* Translated by David Macey. London: Pluto Press, 2005.
——. *Le nouveau jihad en Occident.* Paris: Robert Laffont, 2018.
Lamrabet, Asma. *Islam et femmes: les questions qui fâchent.* Paris: Folio Essais, 2018 [2017].
Le Breton, David. *Disparaître de soi: Une tentation contemporaine.* Paris: Métailié, 2015.
——. *Corps et adolescence.* Brussels: yapaka.be, 2016.
Lefranc, Bérengère. *Un voile: Un certain moi de juin.* Paris: Michalon, 2010.
Le Renard, Amélie. *A Society of Young Women: Opportunities of Place, Power, and Reform in Saudi Arabia.* Translated by Kate Rose. Stanford: Stanford University Press, 2014.
Liogier, Raphaël. "Le voile intégrale comme trend hypermoderne." *Multitudes* 42 (2010): 14-20.
——. *Le mythe d'islamisation: Essai sur une obsession collective.* Paris: Le Seuil, 2012.
Lipovetsky, Gilles. *La troisième femme.* Paris: Folio Gallimard, 1997.
——. *Plaire et toucher: Essai sur la société de séduction.* Paris: Gallimard, 2017.
Mahmood, Saba. *Politics of Piety: The Islamic Revival and the Feminist Subject.* Princeton: Princeton University Press, 2011.
Malik, Maleiha. "De la persécution des hérétiques à la loi sur le voile." *Place publique,* (September-October 2014): 71-75.
Marzouki, Nadia. "La controverse comme transformation du compromis." In *Quand la burqa passe à l'Ouest: Enjeux éthiques, politiques, et juridiques.* Edited

by David Koussens and Olivier Roy. Rennes: Presses Universitaires de Rennes, 2013.
Metcalf, Barbara. "Tablîghî Jamâ'at and Women." In *Travellers in Faith: Studies of the Tablîghî Jamâ'at as a Transnational Islamic Movement for Faith Renewal*. Edited by Muhammad Khalid Masud. Leiden: Brill, 2000.
Moulères, Sandrine. *Les boucs émissaires de la République: Moi, Sandrine, ma vie, mon histoire, ma vérité*. Paris: Michalon, 2010.
Muzzarelli, Maria-Giuseppina. *Histoire du voile: Des origins au foulard islamique*. Paris: Bayard, 2017.
Roy, Olivier. *L'Islam mondialisé*. Paris: Le Seuil, 2003.
———. *La laïcité face à l'islam*. Pluriel: Hachette, 2005.
———. *Islam and Death: The Global Appeal of Islamic State*. Translated by Cynthia Schoch. Oxford: Oxford University Press, 2017.
Scott, Joan Wallach. *The Politics of the Veil*. Princeton: Princeton University Press, 2007.
Sellami, Meryem. *Adolescents voilées: Du corps souillé au corps sacré*. Paris: Hermann, 2014.
Wieviorka, Michel. *Retour au sens: Pour en finir avec le déclinisme*. Paris: Robert Laffont, 2015.

Filmography

De Féo, Agnès. Documentaries produced by Marc Rozenblum:
Mission Tabligh, 52 minutes, 2009.
Sous la burqa, 52 minutes, Sasana Productions, 2010.
Au coeur de Deoband, 26 minutes, Sasana Productions, 2011.
Niqab Hors-la-loi, 52 minutes, Sasana Productions, 2012.
Niqabmania à Tunis, 52 minutes, Sasana Productions, 2013.
La Tunisie et ses femmes salafistes, 26 minutes, lemonde.fr, 2015.
Émilie König vs Ummu Tawwab, 26 minutes, L'Obs, 2016.
Voile interdit, 43 minutes, Sasana Productions and Slate, 2017.

AGNÈS DE FÉO is a sociologist and documentary filmmaker. Since 2008, she has been studying women in the Salafist movement in France and has made eight films on the subject of the niqab. Her previous work, on the Cham community in Vietnam and Cambodia from 2002 to 2012, has resulted in five documentaries as well as a book, *Parlons Cham du Vietnam* (2016).

LINDSAY TURNER is Assistant Professor of English and Creative Writing at Case Western Reserve University. She is the author of two collections of poetry and has translated books by Stéphane Bouquet, Éric Baratay, Souleymane Bachir Diagne, Anne Dufourmantelle, Richard Rechtman, Ryoko Sekiguchi, and others.